Richard&Judy

Wine
Guide

Richard&Judy

Wine Guide

Amanda Ross
Susy Atkins
Jean-Marc Sauboua
Joe Wadsack

Harper Collins *Entertainment*
An Imprint of HarperCollins *Publishers*

HarperCollinsPublishers
77–85 Fulham Palace Road,
Hammersmith, London W6 8JB

www.harpercollins.co.uk

Published by HarperCollins 2005
1 3 5 7 9 8 6 4 2

Photographs
Copyright © Mark Read
With the exception of copyright © Noel Murphy: 1, 10, 16, 39, 65, 82, 106, 133, 159,
190, 193, 214, 237, 259, 283; copyright © Jim Marks: 8; copyright © Amanda Ross: 14–15;
copyright © Frescobaldi family: 26–27; copyright © Aliénor de Malet Roquefort: 74;
copyright © Bodegas Chivite: bottom left 96; copyright © Miguel Hurrioz Ruiz: 148;
copyright © De Bortoli family: top right 180; copyright © Cactus TV: 262

A catalogue record for this book is available from the British Library

ISBN 0 00 722109 6

Set in Scala and Helvetica
Designed and typeset by Smith & Gilmour, London

Printed and bound in Great Britain by Butler & Tanner

To get any of the wine mentioned in this book, or for
more advice, or to join the Wine Club call 0870 420 3844
or visit www.richardandjudywine.co.uk/guide

To Sergio Mottura, a true gentleman,
your passion for wine and love for
your land inspired us to create the
Wine Club and write this book

Contents

Richard and Judy

Many of us have found our hearts sinking and a light beading of perspiration forming on our brows on hearing the words: 'Would sir or madam care to see the wine list?' For some, even the in-flight attendant's, 'Would you prefer the New Zealand Sauvignon or the French Chablis with your meal?' is a poser roughly on a level with, 'Do you consider the early Mayan pottery superior to the later designs?'

The world of wine can often seem shrouded in timeless mystery, ruled by ancient and terrifyingly complex rituals. But, as more and more are discovering, it is in fact rather more like the sphinx without its secret.

This book strips away the many myths and misunderstandings about wine to reveal the simple truths and pleasures of one of mankind's oldest gifts.

Some of the world's leading wine experts come together to describe, without a hint of patronage, how a good wine is grown, harvested, fermented and served. They will also explain how to get the best out of the bottle you have just uncorked – or increasingly these days, uncapped – and how to share what you will learn about tasting and enjoying its contents with family and friends.

Cheers!

How to Use This Book

There's nothing particularly mysterious about a glass of fermented grape juice, but when you hear or read most wine critics eulogising about all those extraordinary aromas, flavours and textures, you feel like you've entered a different and intimidating world with a language all of its own. How can one glass of wine be so very different from another? But think about it – a dry, light, crisp white Sauvignon Blanc, compared to a powerful, mouth-coating, full-bodied red Shiraz . . . and what about the fact that few wines actually taste of grapes, but instead have the character of blackcurrant, gooseberry, lemons or cherries? Not to mention the subtle notes of spice, pepper, cream, vanilla, grass and coconut . . . it's intriguing stuff, this amazing liquid, but its enjoyment doesn't need to be shrouded in mystery and complicated by jargon.

The whole business of wine appreciation is subjective – if you don't like a wine then it's not a good wine – everyone's opinion is valid, but we are going to give you the skills, vocabulary and basic knowledge so you have the confidence to express your opinions in any situation, make sure you get the best wine for your money, and most importantly increase your enjoyment.

It's very hard to fathom the language of wine critics – if you're not tasting the same wine they are, you can have no idea what they are talking about. The unique aspect of this book is that you drink along with the experts, see if you can taste what they taste, and consequently are learning as you go.

Each bottle of wine you crack open should have a clear identity – a flavour of the place it was made, and the climate, grapes and techniques individual to that piece of soil. In each chapter there is a featured bottle of wine that we use as a starting point for all our comparisons and comments so you have something to measure your opinions against. We then give you comparisons with other wines so you can build your knowledge. There's also a profile of different grape varieties. You can get our featured wines in the shops or, most easily, through the Wine Club (details on page 4). There are twelve chapters, so twelve bottles to make the perfect starting point of a 'case' of education!

There's another factor that's crucial to the character of an individual wine – the person who created it. A wine's personality is to a large extent shaped by the winemaker, so we have profiled all of the producers who made the superb set of wines in this book. Each has a fascinating lifestyle and plenty of wise words to say about discovering wine, so through their life story we find out more about the whole winemaking process.

The first half of this book tells you about why the wine in your glass tastes the way it does. There's lots of information on the way it is made – the basic method of turning grapes into wine, of course, but more detail on the top grape varieties, blends of grapes, oak ageing, organic wines, small wineries vs large, climates, soils and so on. We're not going to blind you with science, but will give you the low-down on the simple techniques and natural factors that make your dry white from Italy taste so very different to your fruity rosé from Spain and your rich red from Bordeaux.

In the first part of the book, the focus is on Europe. This is where most of the important winemaking and grape-growing traditions originated centuries back. The ancient Greeks and Egyptians and the Babylonians of Mesopotamia were among the early civilisations making wine thousands of years ago; but in more modern history, it has been the French, Italian and Spanish who have made a particular mark on our wine drinking, as well as the Germans and Portuguese. We've concentrated on important regions in Europe before heading off into the wider world in Part Two.

Scattered throughout the book you'll find tips from our three experts and some simple solutions to some of the everyday problems and queries that you may have. These tips aren't specific to any particular chapter, and you could simply flick through the book and use the tips on their own. Joe Wadsack gives advice on enjoying, appreciating and keeping wine; Susy Atkins' tips focus on matching food and wine, and specific advice for occasions; and Jean-Marc Sauboua gives insight from the grower's perspective in his distinctive French style. Finally, each chapter is rounded off with a 'myth buster' – a great piece of de-mystifying advice that will help you get more out of wine.

Enjoy the journey, that's what wine is all about . . .

Chapter 1
How to Taste Wine, the Harvest, and Red Wine
Featuring Frescobaldi in Tuscany, Italy

How to Taste Wine

Learn to taste wine like a pro and you'll get far more enjoyment from it, which is what this book is all about. Don't imagine all that sniffing, slurping and spitting is pretentious – far from it; it's a great way of releasing as much character as possible from the liquid in your glass. You'll discover far more aroma, texture and flavour.

Here's how to find out for yourself in seconds: pour out half a glass of wine and simply take a sip, deliberately without smelling it first, and swallow it before it has barely touched the sides of your mouth. Think about whether any flavours or aromas came to you afterwards – probably not much.

Now take another sip, but before you do, swirl the liquid around the glass, get your nose close to it and take a big sniff or two. Then swoosh the wine around your mouth before you swallow it. Suddenly, loads more aroma and flavour have been delivered from exactly the same glass of wine. See? So *that's* why those wine pros go through the elaborate tasting process . . .

But actually it isn't that elaborate. Tasting involves three senses – sight, smell and, of course, taste. Let's do it again, but more slowly this time. First off, you *look* at a wine to determine its colour, clarity and density, and to make sure there's nothing floating in it! Appearance counts for a lot – for example, with red wines, a bluey tint indicates a youthful wine, while a brick-brown hue indicates age. With whites, a deep yellow-gold might mean the wine is sweet, or oak-aged, whilst a very pale, watery white usually means the wine will be dry and unoaked.

Now swirl the liquid around to release the aromas – don't worry if you slop a bit over the edge, as wine tasting often gets pretty messy – and try to make as much wine whirl around the glass as possible. Take a big sniff, or a series of small sniffs, and analyse the aroma. Is it fruity or spicy? Rich or light? Which fruits can you smell, and are there other aspects to the perfume, like oakiness, grassiness, perhaps some pepper or a floral note? Try to be imaginative in your descriptions and remember that all tasting notes are highly personal, so you're not looking for what is 'right' or 'wrong'. Just aim to build up a sense of your own reference points – whether the wine seems appealing, fresh, dull or fruity to you.

Do the same with the flavour: take a small sip, or series of small sips, and slosh the wine around your mouth, even dragging a bit of air

through it – the slurping together of liquid and air seems to release the most flavour in a wine. Think about the wine's texture (thick or thin, diluted or rich?) as well as its fruity character, and any extra characteristics like high acidity or creamy oakiness or powerful, chewy structure (from high tannins – don't worry, we'll learn about those later). After you spit it out or swallow it, decide whether the wine has an appealing 'finish' – did it leave any particular flavours lingering in your mouth or was the end rather dull?

Well done, you've finished your first official wine tasting! Try to decide how much you liked the wine overall, whether you would want a second glass of it and how much you'd be prepared to pay for it. Then taste another wine, comparing and contrasting all the time, because it is only by pitching different wines against each other that any of us discovers how wide the range of styles is, and exactly which is best for you in general, on certain occasions, or for certain food matches. Make some notes if it will help you remember everything about the wines you've been tasting.

Finally, try to taste wine sometimes with a friend or group of friends, and compare your reactions to different styles. Remember, no one is right or wrong, but it can be interesting and enlightening to discover what other people thought of a controversial bottle! Another idea is to try the wine 'blind' – get everyone to bring a wine with the label covered up. Unveil the wines only after everyone has tasted and you have given your verdicts – it can be a fun way to challenge your preconceptions about certain wine types and brands, and broaden your horizons.

JOE WADSACK'S EXPERT TIP

Wine Glasses
Wine glasses are an important factor in the enjoyment of wine. Looking round the department stores you'll see a huge range of fancy stemware, but which glasses should a true wine lover plump for? Funnily enough, professional wine tasters reject the fancy styles and opt instead for a plain glass, simply tulip-shaped with a long stem. This is because coloured glass, and even cut crystal, distorts the look of the precious wine – pros like to be able to see the colour and clarity of the liquid in their glass. A slight tulip shape to the bowl of the glass means the aroma is concentrated as it leaves the glass, and a long stem means you can hold it easily to swirl the wine, at the same time keeping your hot fingers away from the bowl where they might warm up the liquid. Choose thin glass – chunky glass doesn't feel so good on the lips. Bigger glasses help separate out the interesting aromas in a wine, making it taste and smell more scented and complex, like large loudspeakers on a stereo do a better job of amplifying music. Remember, you should never fill them more than a third full! Champagne flutes (the tall, thin glasses) are perfect for all fizz.

Red Wines

It doesn't take a genius to work out that red wines are made from red grape varieties, but the method of making red and white wines differs too. Much of the colour, flavour, body and character of red wines come from the skins of the grapes, so winemakers try to extract a little or a lot of this, depending on the style of red they want to make. They often crush the grapes up so the skins (and pips and sometimes stalks) give up a lot of rich flavour and tannin into the liquid. Tannins are a group of organic chemicals found in grape seeds, stems and skins that give wine a lot of its rich structure and body. They can even make wine taste chewy and tough when overdone. Tannins don't sound too tasty, but actually they are essential to the structure of some wines, and they do soften up over time. The winemaker often leaves the solid bits (skins, etc.) in with the juice to stew for a while, so even more flavour and colour comes out. During fermentation the skins tend to float on top, and they can be 'punched' down into the liquid to keep them 'macerating' in the wine (macerating means soaking an ingredient in a liquid, basically stewing the grapes). Sometimes the solid matter is pressed to get the really concentrated juice out of it.

But to make a softer, lighter style of red, one method is to press the fruit very gently so that barely any tannins and gutsy flavour gets into the wine. Winemakers may also do away with crushing or pressing the grapes in the first place, and just let them burst open over time in the fermenting tank without any crushed skins getting in contact with the liquid, which is eventually separated from the solids. This is the technique used in Beaujolais and is known as 'carbonic maceration' – it makes a notably soft, juicy style of red with low tannins.

For more on how white wine is made, see Chapter 2, and for rosé, see Chapter 4.

SUSY ATKINS' EXPERT TIP

Matching Wine and Food
To get the best wine and food matches, you need to use logic and pair like with like. A rich, powerful red goes brilliantly with a hearty peppery meat casserole, but it will overwhelm a cold ham salad; and a light white like Muscadet is no good with a creamy chicken dish, which needs a stronger style – say, a bright, oaky Chardonnay – to stand up to it. Try the lightest, softest reds such as Beaujolais with a rich fish like salmon, and the driest, tangiest whites are wonderful with fresh seafood. Avoid contrasts at all costs, even at the pudding stage: a rich dessert like treacle tart or banofee pie demands a sticky, toffee-coloured, unctuous sweet wine. Match the much more acidic, fresh and clean flavours of fresh fruit puddings with the elegant, featherweight, crisp sweet German Rieslings for a marriage made in heaven. Read our Wine Style Guides throughout the book to help achieve the perfect matches.

The First Stage of Wine Production: The Harvest

If you ever want to spend some time talking to a winemaker, don't attempt it during the harvest! This is usually the busiest time of the year, and getting the grapes in at exactly the right moment can cause a lot of stress. The timing is crucial: the grapes should be ripe enough, but not too ripe or their fresh acidity might be on the wane. The aim is to pick the fruit when the balance between sugar and acidity levels is perfect for the style of wine wanted.

Sometimes this means picking a vineyard's grapes all in one go. Other times the harvest is staggered, so that specific batches of fruit are taken off over time. Watching the weather becomes a vital job, as the grapes are ideally picked during fine dry spells. If rain is predicted, the harvest might be rushed on to get the crop in, and humidity (leading to rot) is another factor the winemakers need to check constantly at this time of the year.

Most harvests take place in September or October in the northern hemisphere and in March or April in the southern hemisphere, although some particular styles of wine mean earlier or later picking. 'Late-harvest' wines are generally sweeter, riper, more honeyed and can be picked throughout the autumn. In Germany, they pick semi-frozen, late-hanging grapes for their famous, luscious Eiswein in November, December or even January. But sparkling wines require sharper juice from the grapes, so fruit for bubbly tends to be picked much earlier in the season when acidity levels are higher.

Most harvesting today is done by machine, although some is still carried out manually, often by casual workers. Hand-picking is especially useful where the vineyards are too steep or have terrain that's otherwise difficult for machines, or when humans are needed to carefully select ripe bunches of fruit or to avoid rotting ones. It is generally more expensive, and that cost might be transferred to the price of the finished wine. Machine-harvesting in very hot spots is sometimes done at night, because the cooler temperatures help the grapes stay fresher as they are transferred to the winery.

Grower Profile Frescobaldi

A great way to begin to understand wine is to get a feel for some individual growers and producers and the different ways they work. If your only experience of wine shopping is in the supermarket, it's easy to imagine that vast multinational companies and impersonal big brands dominate everything in today's wine industry. Far from it! In some corners of Europe there are a few traditional wine dynasties still going strong after hundreds of years. Frescobaldi is one of the most famous, and they produce our example wine for this chapter.

In stunning picture-postcard countryside that is everyone's clichéd ideal of Tuscany, based in beautiful and historic properties, the Frescobaldis produce some of the best wine in the world. This aristocratic family have been prominent in Italian arts, culture and farming for over 900 years. They've long been established in Tuscany, close to Florence and Rome, and at the heart of fine wine production.

In the 11th century, the family lived in Florence at a time when the city was rapidly expanding, and they became important businessmen and bankers, operating silver mines and minting coins. The Frescobaldis made a move into farming, and grape-growing eventually became their

major occupation. Now the family have been making wine in Tuscany for an astonishing thirty generations since the early 14th century, so it really is in their blood! That said, over the years Frescobaldis have also become famous poets, composers and builders, always associating and trading with royalty and the most famous men and women of the day. They are one of the most important families in Italy's history.

Many historical documents reference the family's wines, and by the 16th century we know they were supplying wine to European royal courts, including England's, from their base in Florence. Family archives chart the fascinating history of trade with other countries, and there's even ancient correspondence with the court of King Henry VIII.

In the 19th century, the family land was united with the estates of another group of Florentine aristocrats, the Albizi family. Following Angiolo Frescobaldi's marriage to Leonia degli Albizi in 1863, the two families became one of the biggest landholders in Tuscany. A key figure was Leonia's older brother Vittorio degli Albizi, who started a revolution in Italian wine when he sought out a selection of foreign grape varieties to plant in Tuscany. Today we're used to seeing the same grapes planted all around the world, but in the 19th century, varieties were still only planted in their home lands, and Tuscany would have known few vines apart from its native ones, particularly Sangiovese. So, for Vittorio to import Chardonnay, Pinot Noir, Cabernet Sauvignon and Merlot was a really exciting and innovative move. Sadly, he died before he reached forty, but the family continued Vittorio's progress and carefully monitored his work on their Pomino and Nipozzano estates.

Since this time, the Frescobaldi family have been associated with a forward-thinking, modern approach to wine. They adore Sangiovese and other noble Italian varieties, but have gained a reputation for trying out other vines and blending the Italian grapes with international ones to make inspiring, original styles.

JEAN-MARC SAUBOUA'S EXPERT TIP

What is Terroir?
Have you ever heard the word "terroir"? There is no precise translation for this French word: "terrain" comes nearest but has a less specific, and above all a less emotive connotation. Terroir means the complete package of growing conditions specific to a vineyard or site, which influence the style and quality of the wine that can be produced there. Terroir is composed of topography (altitude, slope and orientation), climate (temperature, sunshine and rainfall), soil and subsoil. For the French, terroir is an article of faith, and the appellation contrôlée system is based on it. Even the New World is looking for special terroir to make special wine. In New Zealand, the terroir of Marlborough produces superb Sauvignon Blanc, and in Australia, the terroir of the Barossa Valley makes for a big, rich Shiraz. In this chapter we've seen the terroir of Tuscany produces Sangiovese. It's like for English roses – some gardens produce better ones than others, so even your own back yard has its own terroir!

In the early 1960s there was an important move – growers started to seek out the best soils for each individual grape variety to get better overall quality for their wine. The Frescobaldis invested heavily in new vineyards with the perfect soils and climate for the grapes they wanted to grow. In just a few years, over 500 hectares of premium vineyards were planted on their estates in the Florence area, and the wineries were modernised with up-to-date equipment. All this was at a time when few winemakers thought especially hard about selecting the right plots for particular vines, and many Italian wineries used traditional, rustic methods of making wine, so it's no surprise Frescobaldi built up an international following for their cutting-edge approach.

The pace of improvement has continued for the family in recent years. In 1989, Frescobaldi bought Castel Giacondo, one of Tuscany's most renowned wine estates, in Montalcino near the city of Sienna. Here they make a delicious example of Brunello di Montalcino, one of the key red wines of Tuscany. In 1995 the family teamed up with the well-known Robert Mondavi winery of California to launch the first-ever joint venture between Italian and American wineries. The wine that resulted, Luce, a Sangiovese and Merlot blend, has been highly acclaimed.

In 2002, Frescobaldi became a shareholder in Tenuta di'Ornellaia, one of Italy's most prestigious wine estates, and in 2005, they bought the entire estate as full owners. Ornellaia, a star of the Bolgheri region, makes one of Italy's most famous red wines, a Bordeaux blend of grapes which has won countless awards. Ornellaia, a 'cult' label coveted by serious collectors, is in many ways now the jewel in the Frescobaldi crown. Today the family has nine wine estates in Tuscany and other parts of Italy, and owns around 1,000 hectares of vines.

The current generation of Frescobaldis is as actively involved in winemaking as ever before. Seven family members currently work in the management of the company – they represent the twenty-ninth and thirtieth generations to make wine. Part of the twenty-ninth generation, Vittorio Frescobaldi has been the president since 1980, taking over completely after his father's death. Vittorio was a driving force behind the moves to modernise the company in the 1960s and '70s.

Vittorio's brothers, Ferdinando and Leonardo, are both vice-presidents of Frescobaldi, and the thirtieth generation is represented by four cousins, one of whom, Lamberto Frescobaldi, takes responsibility for winemaking. Born in Florence in 1963, he graduated from the acclaimed University of California, having specialised in viticulture (the science of grape growing). He joined the family company in 1989.

Lamberto worked closely on the important 'Luce' venture with the Mondavi family, where they cultivate vines in one of the highest altitudes in Montalcino. Lamberto's been credited with making huge improvements in quality with the Frescobaldi wines, and his international contacts have been a great asset to the Italian company. When off duty he's an enthusiastic skier and motorbike rider!

Nowadays the family are all based in Florence, living in apartments between the Palazzo Frescobaldi and Palazzo degli Albizi – a 'palazzo' is literally a palace, which tells you everything about the importance of the two families that were joined by marriage back in the 19th century. The Frescobaldis retain a strong sense of their heritage and maintain family traditions – such as, when a child is born, that very day they lay down wine labelled with the child's name in the cellars. The children then have an incredible souvenir of their birth to enjoy at their coming of age or wedding.

Their personalities are quite diverse but they thrive on a common passion for wine and grapes, and share a continued ambition to push forward the boundaries to find the best vineyards, blends and styles of wine. With so many family members at the helm, Frescobaldi remains a personal and friendly company, miles away from the multinational, industrial image of other wine producers of a similar size. They do welcome outsiders to join them, bringing new perspectives and ideas, but it seems likely that 'The Family' will always continue to do it *their* way!

Grape Variety
Sangiovese

Sangiovese is the most important Italian grape variety in Tuscany, and some would argue it is the quintessential, classic Italian red grape. The Italians have many different native grapes, and also plant a lot of internationally famous varieties, such as Chardonnay and Cabernet, in their vineyards. But Sangiovese remains both popular and well-respected for the important role it plays in producing Chianti and other renowned reds of the country.

The name 'Sangiovese' means, rather poetically, 'blood of Jove'. It is usually a bright ruby colour and combines fresh strawberry and cherry, often with a touch of tea leaf or tobacco leaf and dried herby notes, with a lifted, fresh, tangy finish. Some Italian reds made from Sangiovese are richer and spicier, but generally the style is medium-bodied and fruity, and excellent with a wide range of savoury dishes – its slightly tart, tangy finish cuts through fattiness brilliantly. The famous Tuscan red, Brunello di Montalcino, is made from just one clone of the Sangiovese vine, and in reds labelled Chianti and Vino Nobile di Montepulciano this grape is the main component in a blend with other varieties.

Sometimes Sangiovese is used on its own, and sometimes it's paired with Cabernet Sauvignon to make premium Italian blends. It pops up in other parts of Italy, sometimes under different names, but you will hardly ever see it grown outside Italy, although one or two Californians and South Americans have experimented with it.

Tasting Notes Frescobaldi Pater Sangiovese

Susy Atkins

'A bright garnet-coloured wine, smooth, medium-bodied and food-friendly. There's plenty of strawberry and red-plum fruit flavour bursting out of this wine, and look out for the distinct note of red cherries running through it. It's almost sour cherries too – that slightly tart finish is typically Italian – and there's a subtle hint of toasted nuts.'

Joe Wadsack

'This sort of wine needs to be on every restaurant wine list in the country. It has a lovely meaty, savoury aroma, backed up with tangy, cherry and cranberry fruits. It isn't too heavy either, making it brilliant on its own or with a huge array of foods.'

Jean-Marc Sauboua

'Delicious example of Italian red, with ripe fruit absolutely packed with spices and some mineral characters. Well-balanced with good ripeness and weight. This wine might have some staying power despite its forward style. A touch rustic but there is enough fruit and concentration to warrant short-term cellaring for a couple of years from vintage (the date on the bottle).'

Sangiovese is the essence of Tuscany, the great red grape that goes into fine Chianti. Typically it creates lovely, cherry-scented, vibrant and spicy wines that, not surprisingly, go well with regional Italian cuisine, particularly tomato-based pasta and rich meat dishes. This wine is made by the famous Frescobaldi dynasty, part of the Italian winemaking aristocracy.

Wine Style Guide Medium Bodied Reds

Few people actively dislike this style of wine. What's to dislike? It hits a good balance between rich and light, with plenty of generous red-fruit flavour but also some fresh acidity and a bit of tannin to give it structure. Only those who prefer their reds really powerful and tannic, with less acidity, will be turned off. So if you like our featured Sangiovese, investigate the wonderful world of Italian reds to come up with some similar, intriguing flavours, and look at other medium-bodied, fruity red wines from around the world.

In Italy, try other red wines with a distinctive and unusual local flavour. In the south of the country, Nero d'Avola, Primitivo and Negroamaro grapes all make ripe, rounded, fruity red wines, often with a twist of spice and black pepper. Expect blacker, earthier fruit flavours (forest fruits, blackcurrants), and generally a somewhat more sun-baked style than Sangiovese, but similar wild herby traits and an equally food-friendly character.

Italians make their red wines precisely to go well with food, and another brilliant dinner-party wine is Dolcetto, this time from Piedmont in the north-west. Dolcetto (the name means 'little sweet one') tastes of tangy red cherries and plums and is generally made in a soft, likeable, fairly simple way, but is quite delicious with pasta and tomato sauces.

Another Italian red wine that you should try is Montepulciano – not to be confused with the reds of the town of Montepulciano, which are made mainly from Sangiovese. Montepulciano d'Abruzzo makes lots of popular, quaffable, fruity red in central and south-east Italy. Outside Italy, all sorts of medium-bodied reds will appeal to fans of Sangiovese, including the internationally grown Pinot Noir, which has the fresh strawberry character but a more silky-smooth texture. Try young Pinot Noir from Burgundy, or from Chile, California or New Zealand.

Or try Merlot for more lashings of red-berry fruit. Merlot varies considerably in terms of richness and oaky tannins, but many are medium-bodied fruity reds, which are again versatile with savoury dishes. Try one from Chile or South Africa, Bordeaux or the South of France (Vin de Pays d'Oc). And for sheer good value for money, don't miss the reds of the Côtes-du-Rhône in France. Trade up to Côtes-du-Rhône Villages labels for a better-quality wine, still at a competitive price.

Finally, try three New World wines: South African Pinotage, a rarity outside the Cape, but a signature grape with plenty of fruity character (the variety is a cross between Cinsault and Pinot Noir); Californian Zinfandel, which has bags of pippy raspberry flavour and a sprinkling of black pepper in the mix; and Argentine Malbec, which majors on a ripe, rounded black cherry flavour and is a great 'food' wine, matching steaks and barbecued dishes as well as pasta and pizza. A Malbec is our featured wine in Chapter 12 on page 303.

How to Store Wine

It's hard to know where to keep wine, especially if you haven't got a proper cellar. If you plan to hold on to special bottles, do keep them in the right conditions or they may start to taste flat and dull. But don't think that a cellar is the only place to keep wine well. Just pick a place that's reasonably cool and dark and where your wine won't get knocked about. Wine responds badly to fluctuations in temperature, so never keep it by a radiator, or near the oven! The attic is probably too warm; the garage too cold. Instead, choose the cupboard under the stairs, or any other dark, still place, like an old wardrobe or blanket box, or a shady downstairs cloakroom (turn the radiator off!). We know someone who stacks their wine in a large, unused fireplace and another who parks his bottles under the spare bed! Store the bottles on their sides so the cork stays in contact with the wine (if it doesn't, it may dry out and let air in) and try not to disturb it too much. Remember, cheap and cheerful bottles need drinking up soon after purchase – only fine wines should be kept for more than a few weeks. Jean-Marc's tasting notes tell you when to drink each of our featured wines.

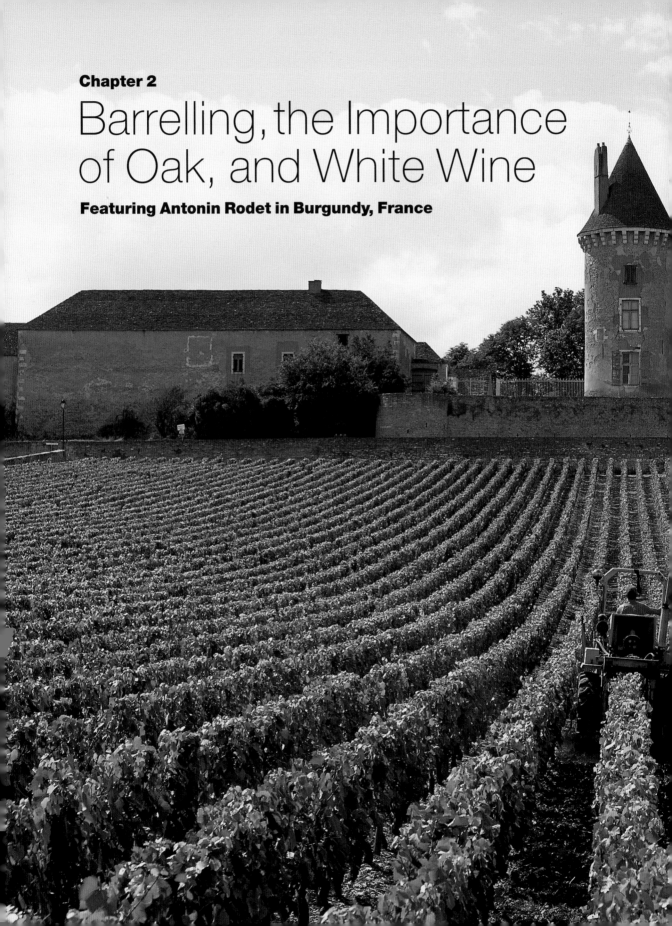

Chapter 2

Barrelling, the Importance of Oak, and White Wine

Featuring Antonin Rodet in Burgundy, France

Barrels and Oak

There's an important relationship between oak and wine and it's one which can make a huge difference to the flavours in your glass. A few people are very prejudiced against oaked wine – they never like even the slightest hint of oak, but most experts agree that if a wine is carefully oaked, it doesn't taste of the wood, but like a wine that has been subtly enhanced.

So what exactly does it mean when a wine is 'oaky'? Put simply, the wine has been fermented and/or aged in oak casks so that the oak container leaches some of its woody character – aroma, flavour, even texture – out into the liquid. The wine will typically taste richer, more vanilla-creamy, sometimes a little wood-spicy or even sawdusty.

Think of it a bit like adding salt and pepper to your food – you don't want the food violently salty or peppery, but you do want a little extra seasoning to set off the food and add subtle shades to it. Oak is a type of seasoning for wine and getting the amount of oaky flavour right is crucial if a wine is to taste good at the end.

Most oaked wines are aged (and whites are sometimes fermented too) in small oak barrels ('barriques' in French) that hold 225 litres. These are normally replaced every two to three years, as new barrels give a stronger flavour to the wine which gradually lessens after each year of use.

So why oak? Oak is not only a great watertight container and a good material to use when a wine needs to be stabilised and clarified, it is also easy to mould into barrels and it gives the right sorts of flavours, aromas and textures to a wine.

There are lots of decisions winemakers can take to give their wines exactly the sort of oaky character they want, as the wood is a versatile tool. First, what type of oak to use. The most commonly found are the highly prized, tight-grained French oak which typically gives a subtle hint of flavour, and American oak which gives a more obvious vanilla character to the wine. Wines that are powerful in style tend to be put into American oak – so Rioja, North and South American and Australian wines are sometimes aged in this.

The size of barrel counts for something too. Larger casks than barriques give less flavour to the wine, as less is in contact with the wood. The age of the oak is also a consideration, as new or used barrels are important to the finished product. Winemakers can get quite detailed here, perhaps ageing some of the wine in new oak and the rest in older barrels, before blending the two parts to get exactly the right balance of flavours. The length of time the wine stays in the barrel is another crucial factor in determining the end result.

There's another subtle difference between barrels: some are 'toasted', which means lightly burned on the inside, which gives a richer, slightly toasty finish to the wine that then sits inside. Winemakers can use heavily toasted barrels, medium-toast or light-toast, or combine use of a few of each to achieve the individual effects they are after.

Of course, they don't have to use oak at all as many wines are completely unoaked. In the 1980s and early 90s, some winemakers – particularly in the newer wine-producing countries – were heavy-handed in their use of oak, giving their wines far too much of this particular seasoning, sometimes to pep up otherwise boring reds and whites. There was too much reliance on heavily toasted barrels, new barrels and extended periods in the barrel, with the result that some wines tasted more of wood than they did of fruit! Although a heavily oaked wine might taste impressive on first sip (it usually has bags of aroma and resinous flavour), it is not often a style of wine you want to *drink* much of! Wine drinkers started recoiling at the smell of sawdusty, creamy, over-rich white wines and over-oaked Chardonnays in particular.

Now the fashion is for lightly oaked wines and winemakers are delivering more subtle, elegant flavours. They have toned down oaky flavours in all but the crudest wineries, and might even just oak-age a small part of the overall volume of wine, blending this oaky element back into the vat before bottling – just as happened with our featured wine in this chapter, the Antonin Rodet. A carefully oaked wine, like this one, has been precisely rounded out with just a hint of extra buttery richness and complexity from the portion of the wine that spent some time inside an oak barrel.

Chardonnays are now appearing which say

JEAN-MARC SAUBOUA'S EXPERT TIP

Why Barrels?
Do you know why winemakers age their wine in barrels? And what the difference between French and American oak is? Let me tell you the secrets of the trade: wine aged in oak barrels leaches out tannin and flavours from the wood and adds it to the tannin from the grapes. American oak has much wider pores than many types of French oak, so more oxygen gets to the wine. The wine therefore ages more quickly, tannins mellow and the fruit develops secondary flavours. American oak also gives out much more overt flavours of vanilla. You will notice this when you smell some Reserva Rioja or New World wines. How a barrel is made and how much toasting it is given also has a big effect on the flavours imparted to a wine. Barrels made with French oak are more complex, discreet and tighter – the story of my life . . . Not!

'unoaked' on the label. The wine world is divided about these, as some experts feel Chardonnay can taste a bit flat and one-dimensional without the extra lick of flavour given to it by some oak (a bit like steak without salt, or white fish without a squeeze of lemon). Others think the natural fruit flavours of white wines should be allowed to sing out on their own. There's no doubt that unoaked whites are currently pretty fashionable, but no one could deny that some of the finest whites in the world come from Burgundy, where generally they *are* aged in oak barrels!

As usual in the world of wine, it's up to you to discover which styles suit you personally, or which occasions suit these styles. Oaky white wines, for example, have the richness and body to stand up to quite hearty food, like salmon in creamy sauces, or rich lobster or crab, but they don't make very refreshing, crisp aperitif wines at parties.

Reds are often aged in oak, which adds extra body and richness, and hints of wood-spice, cream and tannin. Soft light reds such as Beaujolais are typically unoaked, while richer, more powerful styles such as fine red Bordeaux or Californian Cabernet Sauvignon are almost always aged in oak. It works for those wines, but not necessarily for others.

Rioja is interesting as it is barrel-aged for a long time until it has picked up a distinct mellow creaminess. Port and madeira are wood-aged and have an obvious note of oak, and even some Champagnes are aged for a short time in oak barrels, although they never taste overtly oaky, just a bit more full-bodied than usual. Some premium sweet wines are also oak aged.

Not all oaky wines have been inside a barrel, though: oak chips are sometimes used. These are pieces of oak that are dunked into a vat of wine until enough oaky flavour has leached out of them: it's a bit like using a tea-bag! This method is cheaper, perfectly legal and, although the flavours that come out of chips can lack finesse and even taste a little bitter, most 'chipped' wines are perfectly tasty.

An option that lies in-between expensive barrels and cheap chips is to place the staves – the curved pieces of wood that would make the barrel – directly into vats of wine instead of assembling them into barrels, which is obviously more time consuming and expensive. What isn't usually legal, however, is oak essence, a laboratory-concocted additive designed to be a bargain substitute for real wood ageing.

SUSY ATKINS' EXPERT TIP

Difficult Food Matches
If you really want your wine to shine, be sure to tone down "difficult" dishes. Some ingredients are serial wine-killers! Lots of chilli, for example, makes a wine taste of nothing, while vinegar clashes appallingly. Mustards, relishes and pickles can also spell death to wine. So only use these in moderation – a tiny hint of chilli is fine, and a little vinaigrette on your salad should be OK as long as you choose a tangy, crisp wine.

Some other foods are not quite as deadly to wine, but they still cause trouble when you're trying to find a perfect bottle to wash them down with. Egg clashes with tannic reds and very tart, dry whites, so always choose a soft, light red like Pinot Noir or Beaujolais, or a richer, creamier white like Chardonnay or Semillon with any eggy dishes. Asparagus and artichokes are tricky customers that make lots of wines taste horrid – try Sauvignon Blanc with asparagus and dry rosé with artichokes and you'll be fine. Chocolate is spoilt, along with the wine, if you pair it with anything other than very sweet, honeyed styles. Chocoholics should try a chilled sweet Muscat or a Hungarian Tokaji. However, our Argentinian grower in Chapter 12 thinks his red Malbec grape works with chocolate; obviously this is a South American delicacy – try it and see what you think.

Grower Profile
Nadine Gublin at Antonin Rodet

Of all the French wine regions, Burgundy is perhaps the most challenging to get to know – but the most rewarding when you do! It's all to do with the way the vineyards are broken up into small plots owned by different 'domaines' – the ownership is not neatly divided into individual chateaux, like Bordeaux. A domaine might have parcels of vines in lots of different locations and might blend these together or put out a wine made from the fruit of just one bit of land. When you get to taste and compare wines from Burgundy, you will soon see how the flavours subtly change from one plot of land to another.

There is a really special relationship between the Burgundian winemaker and the land. The region has a multitude of small, individual soil-types and 'micro-climates' which create the wide range of Burgundy wines, almost entirely made from Chardonnay for whites and Pinot Noir for reds. Nadine Gublin, the passionate, award-winning winemaker for Antonin Rodet, clearly explains the peculiarities: 'Burgundy is a small viticultural region in surface area, but with a big reputation and a long, important history,' she says. 'The region gives us such a variety of different terroirs to work with, many on a clay-limestone soil, but almost by magic, the wines seem very different from one another. For example, if the vines are grown at the top or the bottom of a hill, the wine is not the same. We can compare the wines clearly because we always use the same grape for reds and the same grape for whites, so we know it is the geography that makes the difference. This is what creates the complexity, the uniqueness, the originality of Burgundy.'

Nadine uses the word 'terroir' here – an almost mystical French term which refers to the particular characteristics of one plot of land – its soil, climate, rainfall, the gradient of its slope – everything about the location that determines the character of the wine in your glass, as explained by Jean-Marc in the last chapter. Terroir is especially important to the winemakers of Burgundy, as they attempt to express the essence of a Chardonnay from, say, Meursault compared with one made in Chablis.

It's an almost intellectual challenge, and one that Nadine relishes. She has been Cellar Master at Antonin Rodet since 1990, after taking a National Diploma of Oenology (winemaking) at Dijon in Burgundy in 1979, and has been working in the region ever since.

She believes the Chardonnay grape can really express itself in Burgundy. 'I'm sure it is one of the best places in the world to grow this grape, thanks to a soil that is perfectly balanced with limestone and clay, vineyards planted on sloping hillsides, and a climate that is neither too hot nor too cold. It is an "easy" grape variety that adapts well in lots of places, but here we can really bring out the effects of terroir on it – for example, Chablis wines grown on mainly limestone soils taste different from those in the Mâconnais, in hotter temperatures and on soils that are richer in clay.'

This shows how fascinating and ever-changing wine can be – it's completely subject to the forces of nature! Grape varieties do not simply taste the same wherever they are planted. Nadine says that she thinks she can often taste more 'heat' and 'oak' in many Chardonnays from other parts of the world. Subtlety in a white wine is obviously important to her and something that comes across in the restrained flavours of the Rodet Chardonnay.

Antonin Rodet is an important, large Burgundian company, dealing in wines from all parts of the region. It owns the Château de Rully and the Château de Mercey in the Hautes Côtes de Beaune, and it sources wines and grapes from many other locations, including the Côtes de Nuits, Mâcon and Chablis. The name for a French company that buys already-made wines to blend, age, bottle and sell is a 'négociant', and

wines in the right conditions but also light and less interesting ones in poor conditions. It's perfectly adapted to Burgundy though – the soils and temperate climate suit it. It needs conditions that are relatively constant, with plenty of light and sun but not excessive heat. Even so, it still demands careful and precise work from the winemaker!'

The use of oak can be a tricky issue, with some people claiming they dislike oaky white wines, but Nadine is sure where she stands for her wines. 'I am very attached to using oak barrels in white and red wines,' she says, as she believes the barrels enhance the character of the wine. But she uses oak cautiously, picking the best coopers (barrel makers) and often only putting a proportion of a wine to age in oak, as with the featured Bourgogne Rodet, only 15% of which is oaked. This part is then blended with the unoaked wine for a more subtle effect. 'Acidity is important too,' she emphasises, 'as it adds a refreshing, thirst-quenching quality.'

Nadine was born in Champagne and still loves that region as well as Burgundy. She also admires the rich reds of the Rhône Valley, especially the big northern Syrahs like Côte-Rôtie and St-Joseph, which taste miles away in flavour from the more elegant, smooth Pinot Noirs she makes. When she cooks, though, she tries to pick dishes that match her beloved Burgundy wines.

'Meats, including poultry, but also rich fish like grilled salmon and tuna, go well with the reds, and so do cheeses and, more surprisingly, black-chocolate desserts!' she says. So much for the Pinot Noirs, what about her white? 'Burgundy's Chardonnays are wonderful with cold ham and terrines, mushroom tart, shellfish, white fish and poultry in cream sauces.' Mouth-watering stuff from someone who has clearly mastered the flavours of one of the great classic wine regions.

JOE WADSACK'S EXPERT TIP

Keeping Unfinished Bottles

I'm often asked about the best way to store unfinished bottles of wine. Well, there are a few gadgets on the market that may help. However, they all work on the principle that if you remove the air from the remaining wine in the bottle, then you will slow down its demise. Some claim to keep wine left in bottles in good nick for up to a fortnight. Not true! Vacuum-pump devices only work reasonably well on bottles that are nearly full, and tend to be more effective on red wines.

A device I often use for storing samples overnight is the Winesaver – this is a can of compressed inert gas – you squirt a couple of blasts of the gas into the bottle and the oxygen is pushed out. But here's my hot tip, simple but very effective: keep the odd empty half or quarter bottle, particularly if they have a screw cap. Don't be proud, old plastic cola bottles will do just as well here. Now, pour the leftovers of the bottle that you're drinking into the smaller plastic one. It's very important that you fill it right to the top, leaving no air in the headspace, then screw up the bottle tightly. Finally, store it in the fridge, whether red or white. The colder a wine is, the slower it will oxidise. A quarter or a third of the bottle is now stored in a new bottle without any air. This will keep for a couple of weeks without spoiling, if kept tightly sealed.

négociants are especially important in Burgundy's wine trade, buying lots of wine from particular parcels of land. Rodet is both a négociant and an independent wine producer.

The company was founded in the 19th century as a wine merchant by Antoine Rodet and his son Antonin. Together with his son-in-law, the Marquis de Jouennes, owner of Château de Chamirey in Mercurey, Antoine turned Rodet into one of the most respected names in Burgundy. The Marquis' own son-in-law, Bertrand Devillard, expanded the business and bought up pieces of vineyard in some of the best parts of the region. Today, Rodet is owned by Champagne house Laurent-Perrier.

All the red wines produced are made with Pinot Noir. 'It's a difficult grape variety, but fascinating,' says Nadine. 'It can give sublime red

Grape Variety
Chardonnay

Winemakers love Chardonnay. It grows easily in almost every grape-growing area of the world and it works well in various different styles, so the producer can choose to use it for sparkling wine, unoaked, crisp, fresh fruity whites or rich oaky, toasty, buttery wines. This grape pops up everywhere, from Burgundy (for many wine lovers, this is its spiritual home and where it makes the best wines) to Spain and Italy, Australia, Chile, South Africa and even China!

The results are impressive. Even 'basic' cheap Chardonnay is almost always at least drinkable and, at the premium end, the finest whites made from this grape are considered among the best in the world. Chardonnay makes up an important part of the classic blend for Champagne and other top sparkling wines, and in cooler climates like Northern Italy and Chablis in northern Burgundy, it produces still wines which have lovely freshness and crispness, with appley flavours and an almost flinty, mineral edge. A versatile grape indeed.

The best richer Chardonnays are enhanced (but not overpowered) by some ageing in oak barrels, emerging with ripe citrus and tropical fruit flavours and complex notes of hazelnuts, cream, vanilla and spice. Don't dismiss Chardonnay if you don't like one particular style of it, as this is a chameleon grape that has many different personalities.

Across them all, though, you find a typically generous fruity streak – this is a grape that gives out loads of ripe fruit flavours (mainly peaches, pineapples and oranges) and in a world that has too many bland, weak whites, three cheers for that!

Burgundy could claim to be the spiritual home of top-class Chardonnay. The best Chardonnays from the region are soft, rich, buttery and subtle, with the potential to age beautifully. The Rodet, from a medal-winning producer, is a wine in this class, with typically rich, mouth-filling citrus flavours and careful barrel-ageing for 15% of the wine, to add a luxurious creaminess.

Tasting Notes Antonin Rodet Bourgogne Chardonnay

Susy Atkins
'This Chardonnay has a pale gold
glint, paler than the richer, heavier style
Chardonnays usually have. It's obviously
fruity from the aroma and the flavour –
the typical pineapple and peach flavours
come through with some greengage. There's
a lovely subtle butteriness on the end that
gives it a long and creamy, rather than
crisp, finish.'

Joe Wadsack
'Not many high-street priced Burgundies
taste anything like the real deal, but this
is a surprise exception. A smell of russet
apples with a wonderfully spicy minerally
hint (breathe in through the nose and it's
like a lungful of seaside air!) leads the way
to a dry but silky, slightly honeyed taste.
A classic match with any posh fish.'

Jean-Marc Sauboua
'Pretty white Burgundy, very approachable,
charming and open. There is a bit of oak
here, but this white also has substantial
peach and some fresh butter and pear
characters. Round but not too big, the silky
texture highlights this appealing Bourgogne.
A Chardonnay you want to drink glass after
glass! Drink now and possibly up to two
years from vintage.'

Wine Style Guide Rich Oaky Whites

The Rodet Chardonnay is in the restrained, subtle style of Chardonnay, because it comes from a relatively cool climate where plenty of acidity is retained in the grapes. But it still has lots of slightly buttery, ripe fruit flavours. If you like this well-balanced but fruity character, do try other ripe, juicy, flavoursome whites.

Viognier is a grape variety to compare and contrast with Chardonnay. It has a distinctive peach and/or apricot aroma and flavour, and a certain richness and weighty texture that reminds some people of Chardonnay. Or rather, good Viognier does – some boring, bland, watery ones exist, so watch out! (See page 281 for a profile of this grape.) Try Viognier from the south of France (Vin de Pays d'Oc) or the Rhône Valley (those from Condrieu are superb but pricey) or pick up an example from the New World – Australia and Argentina make some decent ones.

The Alsace region of north-eastern France makes fruity, unoaked whites, so if it's the juiciness not the oakiness of Chardonnay that you're after, give these a go, especially Alsace's Pinot Gris, which has a ripe, opulent, peachy character. Pinot Blanc from Alsace is a similar, easy-going style of white that is really versatile with food and a good choice for a dinner party.

Also on the hit list if you like fuller, fruitier styles of white are Rieslings from Australia, as these are tangy and bursting with fresh lime juice, and much stronger in flavour and alcohol than lighter, subtler German Rieslings. Do give Aussie Semillon a try too – these wines start off a little grassy and tart when young but develop almost Chardonnay-like richness and ripeness, together with some honeyed, toasty qualities, after a couple of years. Also in a newer wine country, do sample Chenin Blanc from South Africa for its popular, crowd-pleasing apple and guava flavours – it's a great-value party white.

But if you prefer the richly oaked style of Chardonnay, here are some other oaky whites to try. Rioja, in northern Spain, is famous for its red wines, but it also makes some white, traditionally with lots of oaky character from fermentation and ageing in American oak casks. Traditional white Rioja has a distinct creamy, vanilla, almost sawdust flavour, which means most people either love it or loathe it. Always drink it with food as it can stand up to quite rich fish and chicken dishes but is not suitable as an aperitif. If you want even more woody flavour in your wine, try Greek retsina, which is actually made with pine resin. But be warned, it's not for everyone!

Then there are the more elegant oaky whites from Bordeaux. Some of the best white Bordeaux (Graves, for example) are a blend of Sauvignon Blanc and Semillon, aged in oak for a rich seam of spicy wood flavour. A few serious imitations are made elsewhere, particularly in the Margaret River area of Western Australia (see page 176). Look out too for some oaky Viogniers and Semillons, and even some oaky, slightly sweetish Sauvignon Blancs from California, where this style of wine is known as Fumé Blanc.

Above all, though, if you like this wine, try other Chardonnays from as wide a field as possible. Sample other white Burgundies – why not splash out on a Meursault to try a richer Burgundian Chardonnay, or other French Chardonnays from the south of France such as Vin de Pays d'Oc, (try one from the Limoux area), or from other European countries – Austria, Italy and Spain make

particularly impressive Chardonnays. And of course, sample the excellent range from the New World. Not all of them are heavy and rich by any means – New Zealand makes well-balanced fresh styles on both its South and North Islands, but especially in the Marlborough region on the South Island; Australia and California have top-class Chardonnays as well as lots of cheapies; Chile has lovely pure fruity flavours; Argentina and South Africa can be great value. The world really is yours when it comes to this grape.

Then of course there's Champagne and sparkling wine. Chardonnay makes up an important part of the blend in many examples, and if you see the words 'blanc de blancs' on a Champagne label, it means the bubbly has been made with 100% Chardonnay.

Tools of the Trade

Sometimes it seems as though you can spend almost as much on wine gadgets as you can on the bottles themselves! Certainly an avid wine buff can expect to be showered with wine-related gifts at Christmas time – so now you have a new hobby, just wait for the corkscrews, foil cutters, decanters, stoppers, thermometers, coasters and bottle tags to descend on you!

So which ones are genuinely useful and which are merely gimmicks? A good foil cutter is a 'must-have' bit of kit, as is a decent corkscrew. There are some amazingly good (and amazingly expensive) fancy corkscrews around – the best, by Screwpull, have a lever handle on top and look like something a medieval dentist would wield, but they are quick and easy, so a good investment if you regularly open a lot of bottles. Otherwise, pick one with a 'head' and metal arms that push down as you twist, or the reliable, super-cheap 'waiter's friend' model, which is especially good for crumbly corks, and folds up to slip easily into your pocket. Attractive stoppers, coasters and anti-drip collars are not essential, but if you like them, then go ahead, as they look good on the table. Less glamorous, but more useful, is a padded cooling sleeve that lives in the freezer and pops over your bottle to chill it quickly in an emergency. For more on decanters, see Joe's tip on page 70, and glasses on page 19. Don't spend too much on fancy wine accessories and leave yourself short of dosh for the wine itself – a decent bottle to drink is far more important than flash kit!

Chapter 3

Wine Blends and Deciphering Labels

Featuring Alexandre de Malet Roquefort in Bordeaux, France

The Importance of Wine Blending

The single varietal wine – one which has been made entirely from one grape variety – has held sway in the wine world for a good decade now. These wines are simply better known and understood by the average drinker. Most of us are used to enjoying a Chardonnay, say, or a Pinot Grigio, but we understand little about a Rhône blend or the mix of grapes that goes into sparkling wine. Some people are prejudiced against blends due to lack of knowledge, but many of the greatest wines in the world are blends of several different grapes. Champagne is almost always a blend of two or three grapes; port is a blend; Châteauneuf-du-Pape is a blend, as are many of the most luscious dessert wines in the world. In Bordeaux, the art of blending is at its best with the wonderful reds made from Cabernet Sauvignon, Merlot and Cabernet Franc to create 'claret', and the pairing of Sauvignon Blanc and Semillon for impressive dry and sweet whites.

In fact, there are plenty of critics who believe that, on the whole, blended wines are more interesting, complex and complete than single-variety ones. They argue that if you choose the right varieties to blend together, those grapes complement each other so much that you end up with a wine that is more than the sum of its parts. For example, in Bordeaux, the generously fruity, softer Merlot grapes are said to 'fill out' the more austere, tough but powerful Cabernet Sauvignon to make a brilliant partnership, while a sprinkling of another grape, such as Cabernet Franc, brings other subtle nuances into the picture. The truth is that you can get great blends, just as you can get great single-varietal wines, but don't dismiss either – it's just another intriguing facet of this complicated world.

Blended wines perhaps gained a bad reputation because in the past superior grapes were made to go further with poorer, cheaper material. Nowadays, this happens less often, and in fact blending can help ensure quality and consistency. In short, blending gives a winemaker more cards to play with. If one component is slightly under-ripe, for example, a riper element might come from another grape variety in the blend; and brands that rely on a consistent 'house style' from year to year can use blending to smooth out the differences between one vintage and another.

Blending usually means, quite simply, a mix of grape varieties, but it can sometimes refer to other components that make up a wine. A bottle might be made from one grape only, but composed of a blend of different batches of fruit picked at varying times to achieve the correct ripe flavours. It might refer to one wine that has been aged in separate lots – some in oak, some not – then blended together to obtain the right result, as with the Chardonnay in the last chapter. It can also mean a blend of fruit, all one variety but from different areas.

But back to blends of grapes. The French are arguably the master blenders – mainly in Bordeaux, the wider south-west, the deep south and the Rhône Valley – but parts of Italy, Spain and Portugal blend many of their wines. Aussie winemakers love to blend grape varieties together to create their popular Cabernet–Shiraz and Chardonnay–Semillon blends, or emulating the French with similar pairings to those found in Bordeaux. They also regularly blend fruit from across enormously wide tracts of land, shipping in Shiraz from one part of a region to blend with Shiraz from another vineyard growing hundreds of miles away. This willingness to blend is one reason why Aussie wines are so reliable.

The art of blending is taken very seriously indeed in the wine trade, and in the top Bordeaux estates and the Champagne houses further north-east, the master blenders are highly respected. 'Assemblage' is the word used in France to describe the moment when various lots of wine are chosen and used to make up the final blend. Some wines are made up of hundreds of different components, particularly in sparkling wine production. In Bordeaux, each respected chateau spends much time and effort picking the very best lots to make up its top red. The other wines might be blended to make a second label (a less expensive red from the same chateau), or a poor lot might be sold off for a cheaper bottling altogether by another winery.

JOE WADSACK'S EXPERT TIP

Decanting

Decanters look frightfully posh, and buying one may seem to many people to be extravagant indulgence. I mean, what do they do? Actually, decanting is one of the most useful tips in the armoury of a serious wine enthusiast. You should use a decanter (or let's face it, a jug or a vase will do if no one is watching) for one of two reasons. Firstly, if you have a grand old bottle of wine (these days it tends to be a bottle of port) then decanting allows you to pour the wine off the sediment in the bottle, so there aren't any nasty black blobs in the bottom of the glass. With wine being consumed younger and younger, this is less of an issue because sediment tends to occur in quite old wine. The other use for decanting is to aerate the wine fully. This oxidises the wine, which both brings out its aroma and somehow pulls all the flavours in the wine together, making a smoother, more rounded mouthful. Wine Club members have told us that they now decant even the cheapest bottles as they can taste the improvement.

What should you decant then? Well, the clue lies in why you are decanting the wine in the first place. Crisp fresh whites or old delicate red wines don't need it. In fact, it could do more harm than good, blitzing the delicate fruit flavours that are there. A few bits in your wine won't kill you and it seems such a waste to leave anything in the bottle, frankly, especially if it's old and posh. Everything else is a prime target for Joe's flower vase. I even decant young, good-quality Chardonnay. The rule of thumb is, if the wine is likely to improve in the bottle for a few years, it will definitely improve in a decanter.

Deciphering Labels

This is a good time to look at the mysterious way in which the French and other European countries label their wines. At least, it seems mysterious until the basic rules are understood; in fact, it's fairly simple. Whereas most New World countries put grape varieties firmly and clearly on the front label, a lot of European regions don't. Instead, they place more emphasis on place. So a bottle of Bordeaux red typically won't say 'Cabernet' or 'Merlot' on it, but may well have the chateau on the label – the place where the wine was made – and usually the part of Bordeaux where it was made, for example Haut-Médoc. Likewise, a Sancerre is 100% Sauvignon Blanc but you'd be hard-pressed to know it from the label. The important point to the French is that it is a wine from Sancerre in the Loire Valley. Anyway, they expect you to know that white Sancerre is Sauvignon Blanc! Locals would of course have grown up with this sort of regional knowledge.

In Spain, red Rioja says 'Rioja' on the label, not Tempranillo, the grape variety, and most Tuscan reds have no information on the Sangiovese grape that has most likely gone into the wine. Admittedly, this can make life difficult unless you know quite a bit about wine and can be sure that a particular place means a particular grape or blend of grapes. No wonder many of us plump for a label that states the wine is Chardonnay from Maule in Chile!

There's a different philosophy at work here. The Europeans tend to believe the most important factor influencing a wine's character is the soil, climate and culture of the area where it was grown. This is summed up in the French word 'terroir', explained by Jean-Marc on page 28, which is an almost mystical idea of a sense of place expressed in a wine's personality. In Europe, single-vineyard wines are highly revered, as these are meant to capture the essence of a particular, usually small, plot of land.

Few producers in Bordeaux think of their wines as Cabernet–Merlot blends; they think

JEAN-MARC SAUBOUA'S EXPERT TIP

Labelling Blends
What do you think "Estate bottled" means? To have "Estate bottled" on a label, 100% of the wine has to be made from grapes grown on land owned and controlled by the winery located in the viticulture (wine cultivation) area. The winery then crushes and ferments the grapes, finishes, ages and bottles the wine in one continuous operation. The modern fashion for labelling wines by the name of the grape variety has led to increased popularity for single-variety wine – Sauvignon Blanc, Chardonnay, Shiraz, etc. Many of the classic wines in Europe are blends of two or three grape varieties, used to bring excitement and complexity into the wine. Châteauneuf-du-Pape gets the Oscar for the most exciting and complex wine because the blend can include as many as thirteen different grape varieties!

of them as Bordeaux wines or, indeed, wines from a particular part
of Bordeaux which express the character of that place. In the New
World, a grape-variety-mad winemaker would argue that it doesn't
really matter where the wine comes from – soil is just dirt, a medium
in which the fruit grows, while grape variety and hard work in the
winery are what really count.

Today, the two sides are coming together more, with some respected
New World producers now concentrating more on emphasising the
regional character of their wines, while modern producers in some
parts of Europe, especially the South of France and southern Italy,
including Sicily, are putting grape varieties on the label more than ever
before. If you want to drink French wine but like to see grape varieties
displayed on the label, try the Alsace region of north-east France,
which has traditionally bucked the trend, or pick up Languedoc wines –
Vin de Pays d'Oc – which are widely available and generally do
signpost grapes clearly.

Grower Profile
Alexandre de Malet Roquefort

Bordeaux – arguably the most famous wine region in the world – can seem a little intimidating, and so meeting one of the great aristocrats of the region could be downright daunting! How refreshing it is, then, to discover that Alexandre de Malet Roquefort, who made our excellent featured claret, Château du Pin, is very down-to-earth.

'The Malet Roquefort family' sounds as if it might have come straight from the pages of a romantic novel. They are indeed the oldest noble family in St-Emilion, the beautiful, ancient town on the right bank of the Gironde river, where some of the best Merlot in the world is made. Not only is this a family whose roots can be traced back for century after century, it is also one of the most influential winemaking dynasties in the Bordeaux region.

The Malet Roqueforts own Château La Gaffelière, a premier grand cru classé* property that holds many hectares of prime vineyard land,

*On Bordeaux's right bank, St-Emilion's chateaux can apply for the Saint-Emilion or Saint-Emilion grand cru rating. Wineries awarded the latter can submit their wines to be considered for a further award of grand cru classé or premier grand cru classé (subdivided into A and B). There are only two premier grand cru classé As (Châteaux Blanc and Ausone). Château La Gaffelière is a premier grand cru classé B.

mainly planted with Merlot. St-Emilion is the family seat, and has been since the 16th century. In 1969, Count Leo de Malet Roquefort unearthed mosaics depicting vines at the site of Château La Gaffelière which dated from the Gallo-Roman period. This proved that a winemaking culture has been active on the site since the 4th century!

The name La Gaffelière comes from the medieval sickroom once on the site, where lepers ('les gaffets') were cared for. The Malet Roquefort chateau, which dates from the 16th century, is in the heart of St-Emilion, and its architecture charts different tastes and fashions that inspired previous generations of the family – an arched 16th-century kitchen, the 19th-century pigeon house and the 17th- and 18th-century wings which house the chateau's reception rooms.

So much for the history of the undoubtedly grand Malet Roquefort family. Today, as well as producing the famous Château La Gaffelière wines, Alexandre has started a wine-merchant business which buys and sells a range of Bordeaux wines abroad, and he acts as a wine consultant for several estates in the wider Bordeaux area. This is a very modern approach – more like the 'flying winemakers' of Australia, New Zealand and the UK, who touch down in various countries around the world to act as wine consultants for a few weeks at a time, guiding the style that the winery eventually produces, as does our own Jean-Marc Sauboua.

Alexandre does this in Bordeaux, lending his experience to several chateaux over the course of the year. Château du Pin, where our featured claret is made, is in the Entre-Deux-Mers region of Bordeaux, the home for six generations to the Constance family. This is just one of the places Alexandre works. This modern approach to winemaking may sound

surprising for the son of such a traditional French family, but then this is an unusual winemaker – and one who did a lot of his training in Argentina.

'I didn't have any formal training as a *vigneron* in France,' admits Alexandre, 'but then I didn't really need it. I worked in the cellar from a very early age. Holidays in our family were taken to coincide with the harvest so we could lend a hand, and I was often in the cellar or vineyard learning from the adults there. We have a saying here that we are "born in the barrel" and I certainly was!'

But when he was twenty, Alexandre thought it would be good experience to see how wine was made abroad and, in the early 1990s, he settled for three years in the Mendoza region of Argentina, helping to make wine at the French-owned winery Fabre Montmayou, one of the country's best producers.

So how did the fledging winemaker find the Argentinian Cabernets and Merlots, compared to the ones back home? 'It's easier to make wine there!' he jokes. 'All the vintages are good, year after year, and the red wines are all so sunny, rich and ripe.

'But the difficulty with making wine in such a warm climate, is to get the right balance between acidity and alcohol – you can have almost too much alcohol and power in New World wines. It's more of a challenge to make good wine in Bordeaux, especially in poor vintages, but we have the potential for better balance, and ultimately more elegant wines.'

Indeed, it is the graceful, subtle quality that Alexandre prizes most dearly in red Bordeaux. 'Ideally, Bordeaux is not as heavy as other wines,' he says. He doesn't mean he wants to make weak, light red wines in Bordeaux, but those with a fine balance between fruit flavours, acids, alcohol and body. 'It's a question of taste,' he says. 'Lots of other people here are now trying to make dark, powerful wines. But the whole point of Bordeaux is its wonderful balance – the blend of Cabernet Sauvignon and Merlot can provide both structure and fruitiness with restraint and elegance.'

After Bordeaux's wines, he enjoys Rhône reds, white Burgundies and Spanish wine, especially fine Rioja. He remains a fan of Argentina's top bottles, and confesses to drinking a lot of Champagne every December! Now thirty-three, he still lives in St-Emilion, and spends his free time hunting deer and shooting woodcock as well as playing tennis and golf. He recommends drinking the Château du Pin red with red meat – 'beef is best, but lamb is a good match too. Otherwise open it with a good selection of cheeses,' he says.

Despite his sojourn in South America, and his clear love of other classic French wines, Alexandre remains loyal to Bordeaux, as much for its wide range of wines as anything else. 'Here you can get the finest reds, whites and sweet wines, and even the local sparkling wine,' he notes. And he is newly impressed by the quality of the cheaper wines. 'The flavours of inexpensive red Bordeaux have improved a lot,' he says. 'I'm so impressed by the smaller producers and the people spending more time in the vineyard, making less quantity but better quality wines. Australia produces good cheap wine and we have had to raise our quality to compete. And we have! Go into an ordinary French supermarket today and you will find affordable, delicious red Bordeaux, at last!' It's men and women like Alexandre de Malet Roquefort who have made this happen.

SUSY ATKINS' EXPERT TIP

Cooking with Wine
Never use terrible wine in your cooking! There are plenty of people who do – they spot an abandoned, probably faulty, bottle of plonk at the end of a dinner party and keep it for evermore on the windowsill in the kitchen, waiting for the moment when it can be chucked into a stew. By then the already yucky flavour has become completely oxidised! Do yourself a favour and chuck it out. The golden rule for cooking with wine is that if you really don't want to drink it, you shouldn't put it in your cooking either: a tiny bit of that bad flavour is bound to come out in your food. This doesn't mean you have to spend a fortune on wine that's only going to end up in the cooking pot. Use up decent dregs as long as the bottle has not been open for more than a few days, or buy pleasant, fairly cheap, everyday wine for the job. You'll notice the difference, honest!

Grape Variety
Cabernet Sauvignon and Merlot

There are two very important grape varieties blended in the Château du Pin Bordeaux, so it pays to look at both of them. Cabernet Sauvignon and Merlot are, after all, two of the best-loved grapes in the world, capable of making great wines both in blends and all on their own, as well as oceans of everyday quaffing wine.

Cabernet Sauvignon is, for many, the most exciting red grape of all. It makes deeply coloured wines, typically with a rich blackcurrant aroma and flavour, and quite a firm structure – some wines are very rich, powerful and oaky, but they can have intriguing hints of mint, chocolate, cedar wood and the cigar box. New World Cabernets tend to be more richly fruity, with ripe, juicy fruits in the fore. Australia makes some fine, full-bodied Cabs, and very moreish blends with Shiraz; Chile majors on a lush, pure cassis character; and Californian examples can be majestic and hefty and age well for years and years. More about New World Cabernet Sauvignon on page 257.

In Europe, Cabernet plays a starring role in the great wines of Bordeaux and makes more cheap and cheerful ripe reds throughout the south-west and deep south. Both Italy and Spain have some serious examples, often blended with local grapes Sangiovese and Tempranillo.

Merlot is the more juicy, soft and fruity companion, fleshing out Cabernet's more tannic, chewy style. It is typically plummy, sometimes with a fruitcake flavour, and it is the mainstay of some Bordeaux wines, for example the gloriously concentrated top reds of St-Emilion and Pomerol. It makes much simpler, jammy styles elsewhere in France and Europe – look out for good value Eastern European Merlots, and increasingly other countries are trying to make great Merlot. The most successful have been New Zealand, Chile, the USA and South Africa.

Bordeaux is considered the beating heart of the Old World wine trade, and the British have always had a fondness for its red wines, or 'claret' as they are sometimes called. Whilst the top chateaux can command huge prices for their wines for cellaring, the Château du Pin is contrastingly 'modern', fruity and very appealing. Mainly Merlot-based, it combines lovely structure with soft, smooth plum and blackberry fruit flavours – ready for drinking now.

2002

Château DU PIN

BORDEAUX

APPELLATION BORDEAUX CONTRÔLÉE

Sélectionné par la Maison Malet Roquefort

S.C.E.A. VIGNOBLES J.-M. CONSTANS
PROPRIÉTAIRE A SAINT-MARTIAL
GIRONDE · PRODUCE OF FRANCE

Mis en Bouteille
au Château

12% vol · 75 cl

Tasting Notes Château du Pin Bordeaux

Susy Atkins

'A well-balanced wine, by which I mean it has lots of ripe fruit, decent structure and body, with a subtle hint of spice. Plums and fruitcake leap out of the glass – for a claret, it's on the smooth, fruity side. A good introduction to red Bordeaux – a medium-bodied, easy-to-enjoy wine, which would be perfect with the Sunday roast, either poultry or red meat.'

Joe Wadsack

'The simple truth is that the less you pay for a wine, the less likely it is to have those unique traits that make it stand out from the rest. Yet with cedary, green pepper characters and a taste of junipery plummy fruit, there is more raw pleasure in this claret than some wine costing four times the price.'

Jean-Marc Sauboua

'Nice complexity and sense of harmony and finesse, with rich, intense, supple layers of current and plum. Also some black cherry. The aftertaste is long and rich, and the good lingering finish indicates where it's heading. Should improve in the next two years. You can keep for up to four years from vintage.'

Wine Style Guide Blended Reds

Blends of grapes are intriguing and if you like our featured claret, why not take a foray round other well-known blended red wines? Of course, explore the Bordeaux region's wines more fully. Try reds from both left and right banks and compare Cabernet-heavy clarets with Merlot-heavy ones. Do splash out on one or two expensive clarets if you can to truly savour the blending, but you don't have to. The quality of more basic red Bordeaux has improved greatly in recent years, although you should still steer clear of the exceptionally cheap wines from this region.

Explore the rest of Europe's Cabernet blends too. Italian blends of Cabernet with their native Sangiovese can be impressive, and try Spain's Cabernet blends with Tempranillo. You might have to ask a merchant to point out these wines as the label might not give much away, but it's worth the effort so you can compare these blends with the Bordeaux wines – a serious bit of wine tasting that should win you over to blended reds.

In the New World, try the famous blends of Cabernet with Shiraz, both the cheap 'n' cheerful and more expensive. If you get the chance, try a Bordeaux-style blend of Cabernet and Merlot from the Margaret River area of Western Australia (for more on this, see page 176). In South Africa there are fascinating blends of Cabernet and local grape Pinotage, and some with other grapes in the mix.

You'll find more Merlots produced on their own, so taste around the world of Merlot, and be prepared for an enormous variety of flavours, as well as a marked difference between the full-bodied, oaky, richest Merlots and the lightest, simpler, jammy ones. If you have become seriously interested in Bordeaux reds, give Cabernet Franc, the third important grape variety there, more of a whirl by checking out the 100% Cabernet Francs of the Loire Valley. Expect a lighter, tangier style but with plenty of lush raspberry fruit.

Try blended reds that are made of entirely different grapes – in particular, some of the reds of the southern Rhône Valley that are made from a cocktail of varieties. For example, the most famous red wine made here, Châteauneuf-du-Pape, can be produced from no fewer than thirteen varieties, although not all winemakers use the full quota. Grapes used in blends in the Rhône and further south are typically Syrah, Grenache and Mourvèdre, which make heady, rich, sun-baked and very strong reds. Then head to Italy for the famous Chianti, a blend of Sangiovese with other grape varieties – sometimes some white ones are in the mix here, as they are in the Rhône.

Finally, don't forget port, which is a wonderful blend of several Portuguese grape varieties fortified by grape spirit, which stops the fermentation for a strong and sweet result. Exotic-sounding varieties such as Touriga Nacional and Tinta Barocca are grown side by side in the steeply terraced vineyards of the Douro Valley. Some impressive red table wines – unfortified – are now made from the same happy mix of grapes. But anyone truly inspired by blended reds will love the complex and robust flavours in a glass of first-rate, fiery, heart-warming red port!

How Long Can You Keep Opened Wine?

Doesn't your heart sink when you go to someone's house and they pull out a dusty old bottle of opened wine and offer you a glass? Just how long has that bottle been festering at the back of the drinks cabinet? The fact is that wine goes 'off' surprisingly quickly – unfortunately, as soon as air gets to it. It's a bit like biting into an apple and leaving it in the sun – it quickly turns brown. Wine oxidises in the same way, losing its fresh, crisp flavour, tasting tired, flat and rough. So here are the rules you should follow for the perfect drinking-up time:

If you open a bottle of light, easy-drinking white, rosé or soft red, then finish it in two days. Reseal the bottle as soon as you can between servings and keep it in a cool, dark place (or the fridge, in the case of white or rosé). The wine will start to taste a bit 'off' after two days, so ditch it. Rosé is especially vulnerable so drink it up within one or two days. Richer whites might stay OK for two to three days, and very powerful reds might even last three to four days, but they will start to taste much more mellow, soft and less fruity by this time. Dry pale sherry and light pudding wines need finishing within a week (keep them in the fridge); richer sherries, madeiras and ports might keep for two to three weeks – not until next Christmas! Old wine that's gone off shouldn't be used for cooking unless you want to spoil the taste of the food. You can buy useful gadgets to prolong the life of opened wine – see Joe's tip on page 57.

Chapter 4
Rosé
Featuring the Chivite Family in Navarra, Spain

Why is Rosé Important Now?

Styles of wine certainly go in and out of fashion. Rosé has recently rushed back in vogue after years of being widely considered a rather naff, weedy drink. Some wine shops are now reporting sales of rosé trebling year on year! Their shelves certainly glint with plenty of lovely bright pink bottles, when only a short while ago there were just one or two sad rosés gathering dust in the corner.

It's great news that pink wine is finally being appreciated. A glass of young, well-made rosé is a joy, especially if it comes well-chilled on a summer's day. Rosé comes in a wide range of styles (more of which later), but across the board, it should always taste fresh, crisp and fruity, and it should have an enticing aroma of red berries – think strawberries, raspberries, cranberries and rosehip cordial. This is perfect hot-weather wine.

The problem in the past was that too many rosés lacked this vibrant, refreshing character. Badly made rosés taste bland, with barely any of those two crucial ingredients: crisp acidity and juicy fruit flavour. Ten years ago, not only were there too many tired, bland pink wines in the shops, but the majority of them were over-sweet, while masquerading as dry. The sugariness was just about the only distinctive flavour in the glass! No wonder rosé was seen as a second-rate type of wine.

So what has changed? Happily, many winemakers have started to take rosé on as a serious task, creating more time and effort to make ripe, tangy, appealing modern wines. They are using better grape varieties for their rosés, making the most of modern winery equipment, to create a wonderfully fruity, aromatic but dry style of pink wine. We have really taken to the new wave of rosés, and this whole group of wines is more popular than ever before.

How Rosé is Made

Rosé is usually made with 100% red grapes. Notice how the juice of a red grape is clear – the colour is in the skins. That's why a red grape such as Pinot Noir can be so important in the blend for white sparkling wine, as only the juice is used. In rosé winemaking, the crushed grapes are left together with the juice for a period of time, so that the colour from the squashed skins leaches out and stains the clear juice.

The winemaker can choose how much time the juice spends soaking (macerating) with the skins, and therefore how much colour, tannin and flavour the wine picks up from this solid matter. The juice might be run off almost straight away. If it's done very quickly after a short maceration, this is known in France as 'saignée' – meaning 'bled' – the free-running juices from the newly crushed grapes are collected and fermented for a delicate, fresh, pale-pink wine.

Often, though, the skins remain floating in the juice for a number of hours, even for a day or two. The length of time chosen depends partly on the style of rosé wanted, and partly on the natural colouring in each grape variety – some reds have a richer natural pigment than others. A rosé made from Grenache, like our Spanish 'rosado' (featured in this chapter), is probably macerated for around eight hours, although this will vary from vintage to vintage and from one batch of grapes to another, as all batches are different. The stained liquid is then separated by draining or pressing the skins, and it's fermented just like a white wine.

Some rosé champagne is made by blending red wine with white. But generally with rosé wine, the maceration process is by far the most common.

Countries and Styles

Rosés range widely in character, colour and flavour. Your pink might be just that – a vivid cerise colour – or it might be a deeper garnet hue, or orangey-peachy, or barely pink at all. The palest pinks are really off-white. These 'blush' wines, popular in America, are usually sweetish and unexciting. They are made with almost no maceration. Luckily, the Californians are now also making richer, riper and fruitier rosés, deep pink in colour with pretty high levels of alcohol. These wines are almost like light reds.

The Australians are also creating powerful, gutsy rosés and are enjoying success with this no-nonsense, bright and ballsy style of pink. Most are made from Grenache grapes.

Chile and Argentina make slightly more crisp, light wines, but most New World rosés are on the rich side, as are the pink wines of the hotter parts of France. Provence has a special tradition of making rosé – it's said that the Provencals can't bear to miss out on their beloved red wine when the weather gets hot, so they switch to rosé instead of white! You might see some of these wines in strange, traditional, skittle-shaped bottles. The best are delightfully juicy and ripe.

Another very warm part of France, the southern Rhône Valley, makes rosé too – Tavel and Lirac are the specific areas and the words that will stand out on the labels. These are also ripe, powerful and fairly serious, as far as rosé is ever powerful or serious! Southern French rosés are generally made from Grenache, Syrah and Cinsault or blends of these three grapes. Look out for rich creamy notes and even a hint of spice in them.

The cooler the climate, the lighter the style of pink wine in Europe. Head up from the south of France and you'll encounter the medium-bodied, fresh and succulent pink wines of Bordeaux, mainly made from Merlot and generally good quality. Basic pink table wine is made in lots

SUSY ATKINS' EXPERT TIP

Wine and Seasons
For the best wine moments, think seasonally. Those very light, crisp, ethereal dry whites and rosés, ideal out on the terrace on a hot summer's day, just don't work as well at the Christmas knees-up! Move towards richer, fruitier, possibly oakier styles of white and reds when the cold weather blows in, and ditch light rosé altogether. Likewise, forget heavy reds when the spring comes. Now's the time to switch to soft, succulent, strawberryish reds, perhaps chilling them lightly before serving. And of course, spring's the time to get out those aromatic tangy dry whites again! Switching styles with the seasons also means the wine will suit the dishes of the moment too – lighter wines suit summer cooking; heavier styles suit 'winter-warmer' food. Our preferences for certain styles of wine at certain times of the year explains partly why bottles brought back from holiday often don't taste good several weeks later. What seems so delicious on a Greek beach at sunset in August just isn't going to have the same effect on a cold, dark night at home in October. The other reason holiday wines often disappoint is they don't last long – fragile whites, rosés and super-cheap, light reds are meant to be enjoyed soon after bottling.

of French regions, and enjoyed locally rather than exported, but the other important area for rosé is the Loire Valley, further north, where a more delicate, crisp style is found. Quality varies here – Rosé d'Anjou, made from local variety Grolleau, can be a bit insipid and sweet, although to be fair it has recently seemed fresher and more appealing. But for more serious, fruity yet dry rosé, try Cabernet d'Anjou, made from Cabernet Franc grapes, or Rosé de Loire or wines labelled Cabernet Rosé.

Italy makes a few pleasant rosés – Italians call it 'rosato' – and Eastern Europe occasionally comes up with a decent pink. Portugal is famous for the off-dry, spritzy Mateus Rosé, so fashionable in the '70s; it isn't as popular as it used to be, but there are still some fans. Or try the more modern Portuguese pink coming from the Bairrada region.

After France, Spain is the other big European source of rosé, and as our featured Chivite wine shows, Spain creates aromatic, bright, mouth-watering wines, usually with a red cherry and raspberry flavour and clean acidity on the finish. The best come from the Navarra and Rioja regions and are made mainly from Garnacha (Grenache), but look out for others from Somontano, Utiel-Requena or Valencia.

JOE WADSACK'S EXPERT TIP

Describing your Tastes
I remember working in a wine store and being asked what type of red wine the gentleman in front of me should drink. He said that his doctor had insisted that he should drink more red wine to help rehabilitate his heart. I asked him what sort of wine he liked. "Red? Alcoholic? How should I know?" was his response. I gave him a bottle of Beaujolais because it seemed like a good place to start him off. He returned the same day before I closed the shop to say that he thought that the wine was thin, sour and dry, and that it lacked fruity flavour, and he wanted to change it. The point is that, from his complaint, I was able to recommend a wine that was fuller-bodied, lower in acid and riper. I replaced it with a Barossa Shiraz from Australia. He has been drinking it ever since, and still does fifteen years later. Ask anyone to describe a wine that they like and they don't know where to start. Ask them to describe a wine that they hate, and they suddenly turn into James Joyce. The moral? When asking for advice in a wine shop, tell them what you *don't* like, and they will be much better equipped to help you.

Sparkling Rosé

Sparkling pink wine can be delicious, offering more red-fruit flavours than white fizz. Of course, with its vivacious frothy character and pretty colour, it does make a special drink for romantic occasions. Look for the word 'brut' (dry) on the label for a dry pink fizz – the most suitable aperitif style.

Champagne producers are allowed to blend red and white wine together to make their pink bubbly, and many of them do. The most important grape for sparkling pink is Pinot Noir, both in Champagne and in other fine wine regions around the world. There are impressive or good-value pink sparklers being made in California, Australia, New Zealand and Spain, as well as in France.

The Golden Rules of Pink Drink

When you think pink, remember 'cold, fresh, and quick'! 'Cold' means *always, always* serve pink wine well chilled – it really brings out the tangy succulence of the wine and makes it taste more refreshing. 'Fresh' means young – rosé is a fragile style of wine which loses its fresh fruity character after a short time in the bottle, so pick a youthful wine. Always aim for the most recent vintage you can and use a shop with a high turnover to avoid any bottles that have been languishing on the shelves under hot lights. 'Quick' means drink it up! Don't keep rosé once it's been opened for more than a day or two. Keep the resealed bottle in the fridge between servings and chuck it if you don't finish it in forty-eight hours. Given the delectable modern rosés around today, this should not be a problem!

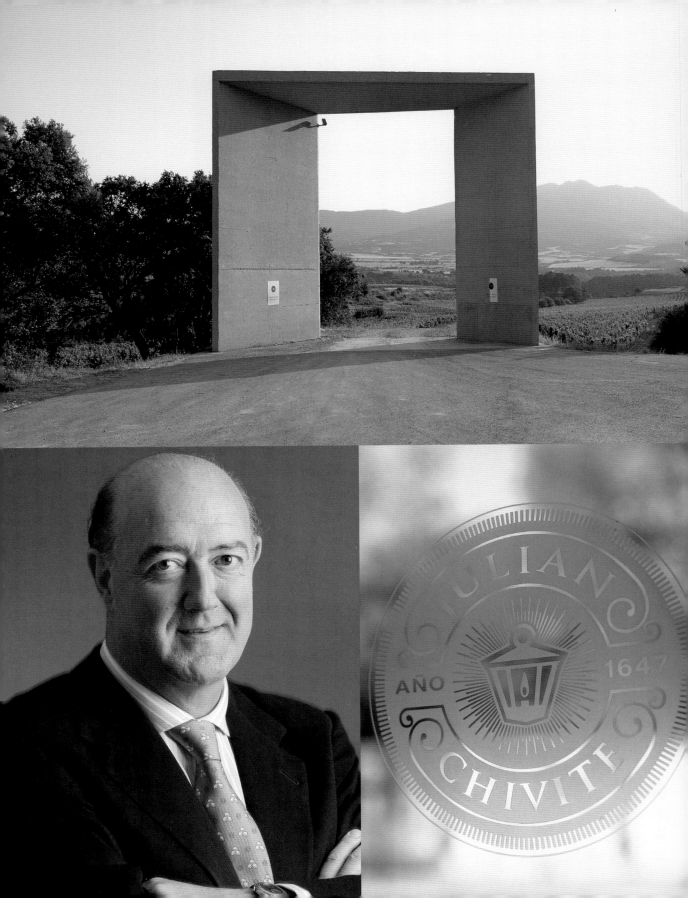

Grower Profile Julian Chivite

Rioja may relish the title of 'most famous wine region in Spain', but it needs to watch its back! Several other areas of the country have started to compete recently, modernising their wineries and coming up with serious reds, whites and rosés. From Priorato in the mountainous north-east (newly acclaimed for giant, tannic red wines), to Ribera del Duero further west (serious, oaky reds) and Rueda, near the Portuguese border (zesty, fresh whites), Spain's other regions are catching up fast. It's no longer accurate to say Rioja is the only star.

One of the most exciting places to emerge is Navarra, which sits right beside Rioja on its north-east border. Once Navarra's winemakers stood very firmly in the shadow of the great Rioja wine estates, but now this part of Spain is home to truly impressive, state-of-the-art operations, the best of which make succulent reds, mainly from local grapes Tempranillo and Garnacha, creamy and ripe Chardonnay, and moreish, refreshing rosé – the style of wine for which the region is most famous.

Many believe Navarra makes the best pink wine in Spain. Certainly this is an area which now gleams with modern equipment – stainless steel, temperature-controlled tanks in award-winning architect-designed wineries. And this sort of high-tech kit is perfect for producing fresh, fruity, modern rosés – miles away from the sort of tired, bland pink wines that used to crowd out the shop shelves. In general, Navarra has edged ahead of some other regions – it is even home to a government-sponsored experimental winery called Evena, where many of the latest developments are tried out.

Ask any expert on Spanish wine and they will tell you that one of the most impressive modern wineries in Navarra is Julian Chivite. A visitor to the main Chivite 'bodega' (Spanish for winery) might imagine the company was set up in recent times – the bodega was fitted with the latest technology in 1990 and is squeaky clean and gleaming bright with new equipment, a bit like a stylish Australian or Californian winery.

In fact, Chivite is a family business that dates back to 1647. A document exists dating from that year in which a Juan Chivite Frias and his sister-in-law applied for a loan against a guarantee of a vineyard and winery with a capacity for 'up to 150 earthenware casks'. Hardly the modern image the firm has now, but proof of an astonishingly long winemaking legacy.

Since then, the winery has passed down neatly through the generations from Juan Chivite Navascues (1678) to Joseph Chivite Navascues (1709) and Juan Chivite Hernandez (1779). In 1860, Chivite wines became some of the first Spanish bottles to be exported, when Claudio Chivite Randez started to trade with France – now the winery exports to forty-eight countries!

It's hard to imagine the French embracing Spanish wine – after all, France would have considered itself the most famous wine-producing nation in Europe in the 19th century. Rioja, and especially Navarra, are not so far from Bordeaux, the great wine region of south-west France, so how did Chivite make this important breakthrough?

The trade with France came about because of a terrible fungal disease called oidium, which wiped out much of the French grape harvest in 1860. Then France's problems got considerably worse. For the rest of the century, its all-important wine trade suffered appallingly as the vine louse phylloxera invaded the vineyards. Phylloxera can be disastrous to vines which have no resistance – this small yellow bug attacks the root system of the grape vine and eventually kills it. At the time, there was no known cure (now many vulnerable vines are grafted on to resistant rootstock).

The effects on the French vineyards in the 19th century were devastating and some wine merchants were forced to take drastic action. The French wine traders, and particularly those in Bordeaux, became desperate to buy wine from nearby northern Spain. France's misfortune became Spain's opportunity, and the Chivite family seized it with both hands.

The company became even more well known under Felix Chivite Frances, who set up an office in Bilbao, by now an important centre of the Spanish wine trade. Exporting wine became a crucial part of the business. On Felix's death in 1928, his son, Julian Chivite Marco, took over and he was a key figure in the important modernisation of the winery through much of the 20th century. Julian died in 1997, and today the eleventh generation of the Chivite family is still developing the company. Three of Julian Chivite Marco's children now work there – Julian Chivite is chief executive, his brother Carlos is the financial manager and another brother, Fernando, is the winemaker.

As well as upgrading their own winery buildings, the family bought the historic estate of Senorio de Arinzano in 1988 and restored it to its former glory, putting in a brand new winery designed by a celebrated Navarran architect. It has been described by John Radford, the UK's leading authority on Spanish wine, as 'a showpiece of ancient and modern Navarra' – indeed it was opened by the King of Spain, Juan Carlos, himself a fan of the Chivite Rosé, who served it to our own Queen Elizabeth!

This visionary winery is now firmly placed in Spain's top ten and has been voted Best Spanish Producer at the International Wine and Spirit Competition. They endeavour to be environmentally friendly and 200 hectares of the winery are a wildlife reserve set up with the World Wildlife Fund.

And that's an accurate image of this family wine company – an unusual meeting of the ancient and traditional with the highly modern and progressive. Chivite's wines are typically very fresh, fruity and elegant – they sing out with bright, clean fruit flavours in a way that can be described as very modern. The Gran Feudo range from Chivite is considered great value for money and our featured wine, Gran Feudo Rosé, is one of Spain's most popular and well-respected pink wines. If you become a fan of Chivite, do try the 125 Coleccion range too – more expensive collector's bottles from a great family firm.

JEAN-MARC SAUBOUA'S EXPERT TIP

Best Picking
Traditional grape harvesting is done by hand, but now there are machines which will do the job much faster. Machines don't get tired, don't get paid overtime and never go on strike – why aren't the grape-pickers worried? Because you can't get better than handpicked grapes. Like haute couture, the world's finest estates still choose to do everything by hand. This is because each individual bunch of grapes will be assessed and selected before making it to the cellar. And of course, machines can't always make it up steep hillsides. In certain cases, some aromatic grapes, such as Sauvignon Blanc, benefit from being harvested at night and taken to the cellar as quickly as possible, to preserve the fresh, crisp taste that characterises this wine. As a winemaker, crafting a wide range of wines, I've used both methods and each has its merits.

Grape Variety
Grenache

Our featured rosé is made mostly from Garnacha, most commonly known as Grenache and, for many, an unsung hero of wine. In fact, it used to be regarded as nothing more than a 'work-horse' grape to the French and Spanish, not to mention the Australians – the sort of variety that was used to churn out oceans of cheap red and rosé, generally enjoyed in bars and restaurants in carafes, or sold at knock-down prices from the local co-operative winery. If you go on holiday in southern France or Spain, chances are you've enjoyed a glass or two of pink or red Grenache without knowing it, as the grape is rarely named on the label.

Some winemakers are starting to take this grape more seriously these days, and it can be found making concentrated, robust reds in Catalonia, Spain and southern France, and is one of the most important grapes in the southern Rhône blends.

This is a versatile grape that makes lots of different styles of wine, not only crisp rosé and rich red, but jammy, simple lighter red and even sweet red wines in the south of France (Banyuls and Maury). Its main characteristic is a big-hearted, generous fruity nature with lots of plum, cherry and raspberry fruit, but it doesn't have a firm structure and can lack body and finesse. It makes a good blend for ripe, slightly spicy reds in the south of France with the Syrah and Mourvèdre grapes.

New World winemakers have started to make more impressive, gutsy red Grenache, especially in Australia and California. It sometimes appears on its own, but sometimes with other southern French grapes. In Australia the blend of Grenache, Shiraz and Mourvèdre is currently very successful and trendy, and is commonly known as GSM!

Rosé has rocketed in popularity in the UK and is now drunk all year round by people looking for refreshing but subtle fruit flavours. The Chivite family really are top Spanish winemakers and their Gran Feudo is made from the Garnacha (Grenache) grape, giving it aromas of strawberries and redcurrants and a delightfully clean, crisp finish. This wine is produced to be drunk when bought.

Tasting Notes
Bodegas Chivite Gran Feudo Rosé

Susy Atkins

'It's hard to imagine a more appealing wine to look at and sniff – it's a vivacious bright pink and smells of fresh raspberries and cranberries. Rosé should always invite you in with its colour and aroma, and this does! Look out for a fresh, red-berry flavour and a succulent, tangy finish too. I want tapas-style dishes with this – cold ham, prawns, salty nuts, olives . . . '

Joe Wadsack

'Spanish rosé like this is all about ripe, juicy fruit. This one smells of fresh strawberries and tastes like a redcurrant sorbet. It's remarkably versatile in the grub department too. Great with trout or salmon, and frankly the only thing to throw back with a paëlla.'

Jean-Marc Sauboua

'Wonderful clarity and vivid colour set the stage for this floral and boiled sweet rosé. The expression of the Garnacha/ Grenache is pure and nicely focused, the nose and palate are bursting with fresh strawberry. I love it! The mouthwatering finish draws you back, a real crowd pleaser. Drink now, don't keep for more than a year.'

Wine Style Guide Rosé

A few years ago, the general quality of rosé was pretty depressing – how things have changed! Today, if you like the Chivite rosé you're in luck, as there's a wonderfully wide range of other delicious dry pinks waiting to be tasted. Do sample plenty and be aware that sugar levels still vary a lot, so you are bound to crack open some rosés that taste bone-dry and some with a more luscious, sweet note. Some are much richer and more powerful, whereas others are pale, light and subtle – or bland, according to your taste! Try other rosés from Spain, especially examples from other regions, particularly Rioja. Head over the border to France, sampling some of the wines described in this chapter. The pinks of Provence, Rhône, Bordeaux and the Loire are a must, and try to compare and contrast them, bearing in mind that different grape varieties are used across France and styles vary considerably as you head from the warm south – Provence – to the cooler north – Loire.

It's also essential to try pink wines from California and Australia, as it's fascinating to see how the newer wine-producing countries are turning out their rosé, often using Grenache and other varieties popular in Europe. When you buy pink wine from California or Australia, note the alcohol level on the label, as it may be relatively high, and think about whether the flavours are different – or perhaps the texture is not the same. Rosé from hot areas can sometimes taste richer

and 'weightier' than cooler climate pinks.

If you find you love pink wine, do try sparkling versions, especially Champagne for a treat! Note the different flavours compared with white fizz – you should expect more red-berry aromas and flavours, and perhaps a hint of strawberries and cream. Try pink fizz from other parts of the world too, especially Australia, New Zealand and California, which each make a few examples.

And why not sample a few very light red wines and compare them with rosé? Beaujolais, Australian Tarrango, some lighter Italian reds such as Bardolino and the simplest Pinot Noirs would all be good contenders. Do you conclude that rosé is more like a light red, or does it have more in common with white wine? There's no right or wrong here, but it makes a good starting point for a tasting session!

Once you've tasted round the subject, why not try some simple food and wine matching with rosé? Too often rosé is enjoyed on its own, typically on a hot summer's day, with little thought given to the great partner it can make with food. The Spanish know differently, and quaff rosé in tapas bars with a range of light savoury snacks like cold ham (jamon), fresh prawns, olives and tortillas. Pink wine is so versatile with food – try fresh white fish and seafood, pasta with a creamy sauce or lightly spiced food, such as Thai fishcakes, with it too. Sweeter rosés are great with fresh berry fruits.

What is Corked Wine?

Faulty wine is a huge disappointment – price is no guarantee, it can affect a fancy, expensive bottle as well as a cheapie. So what exactly is corked wine? It's not when a wine has cork pieces floating in it – that's just due to a crumbly cork and won't affect the flavour. Corked wine has been tainted by a mouldy cork, which has left a musty, dank smell and flavour in the wine, and is no fault of the grower (see Jean-Marc's tip on page 146). A bad case of cork taint is pretty easy to spot; a mild case just deadens and flattens the fresh fruity character of the wine. The *Which? Wine Guide* reckons that 'roughly 5% of all corks are affected'. The unreliability of cork is why there is a move to screw caps on bottles (see page 147). Always be on your guard for corked wine – when you smell and taste a new wine that has been bottled under cork, it should be the first thing you check for. If you're not sure whether the wine is corked, swoosh it about in the glass for a while, as contact with air increases the 'corky' character. Look out too for oxidised wine – when a wine is oxidised, it has been exposed to air or stored somewhere too hot and lost its fresh fruit flavour. It will smell nutty and look a bit faded and brown, sometimes tasting a little like old sherry. It doesn't matter in a sherry or madeira because that is the style they rely on for their typical character, but in a table wine oxidation is not a good thing. Now you know the characteristics, if you spot either in a restaurant have the confidence to send the wine back.

Chapter 5
Bespoke Growers and Organic Production

Featuring Sergio Mottura in Civitella D'Agliano, Italy

Small-Scale Winemaking

Until now we've looked at large modern wineries that turn out hundreds of thousands of bottles each year. Now let's take a look at something different – a small, family-run winery in Italy, headed by Sergio Mottura, that makes only 120,000 bottles each year and has a passionate commitment to small-scale, hand-crafted wine, making use of traditional local grape varieties.

There are some definite advantages to small-scale wineries. The winemaker can be really 'hands-on', working closely (and, often, lovingly) with a small patch of vines and a compact winery to produce exactly the sort of flavours he or she wants. These producers often have a strong sense of place and are extremely committed to capturing the flavours and aromas that are specific to their region. The best smaller winemakers put a lot of time into creating these bespoke wines, quite the opposite from the mass production of some big wineries, where fruit might be brought in from a wide region to be blended in huge vats, producing flavours which are not typical of any one small area.

But the smaller producer has to work especially hard to compete on price, as he has no 'economies of scale'. His wines might cost slightly more and might not taste as consistent from year to year as the wines from a big company. That's because a larger producer can call up more fruit from further afield to cope with any problems or shortfalls; they simply have more resources than a small family concern. A poor harvest or a slump in sales can spell disaster for a family-run wine business, so many of these winemakers rely on other forms of income besides their wine (like the Motturas' hotel and their specially hosted wine dinners).

Happily, many serious wine lovers really do appreciate the work of small-scale producers. Even if you start off drinking the big brands of wine, as you grow more passionate about the subject you may well realise that it's often the smaller producers, working closely with a particular patch of vines, who can coax the most interesting and unique flavours into a bottle. Sometimes the smaller producers can make the bigger mass-produced bottles taste a bit dull and uniform.

Organic Wine

It often follows that where you find a smaller-scale, hands-on winemaker, you also find organic wine. Producers like Sergio Mottura, who are dedicated to their own vineyards, are especially keen on natural methods of growing grapes. They believe it's not only good for the soil, the plants and the environment, but that it also creates better wine.

So what, exactly, is organic wine? There are plenty of myths about the subject, including the idea that organic wines are made not from grapes but from dandelions, goat droppings or turnip tops! In fact, it's quite simple. Organic wine is made from organically grown grapes, which means no fungicides, pesticides or herbicides are used in the vineyards, and no artificial fertilisers are added to the soils. Otherwise, almost everything is the same whether your wine is organic or non-organic – the grape varieties are the same, the winery methods are pretty much the same, and frankly the results are pretty similar; there are bad organic wines and there are good ones, just as with 'normal' wines. That's usually down to the winemaker.

Fervent supporters of organic wines agree with the producer that these wines taste slightly better – more intense and 'true' to the grape varieties used, a bit like some say organic carrots taste better, more 'carroty', than non-organic ones. Make up your own mind by tasting organic bottles. Consider that an organic grape grower may spend more time caring for their vines, which might affect the results. But then without the use of sprays in bad conditions, the grapes can suffer too.

Where the real benefits of organic grape growing can be seen is in the land. Organic vineyards don't suffer from a build-up of chemical residues in the soil. They teem with natural wildlife, with abundant birds and insects living in them. They look beautiful too, as organic growers often encourage wild grasses and flowers to grow between the rows

JEAN-MARC SAUBOUA'S EXPERT TIP

Biodynamism
Are winemakers all bonkers? As a profession, winemaking seems to attract more than its share of eccentrics. You could even argue that being a corkscrew short of a picnic basket is an essential qualification for a job that requires you to spend a lot of time in dark, enclosed spaces with nothing but fermented juice for company. And now some organic wine winemakers are going even further with 'biodynamism'. This is a system of viticulture based on planetary movements inspired by the writings of the Austrian philosopher (and teetotaller!) Rudolf Steiner about "spiritual science" – for example, you can only do your pruning when Mars is in conjunction with Uranus! It's an increasingly popular form of viticulture where the use of various vineyard preparations such as dung, camomile or nettles help to harness the "four levels of matter" (heat, light, water and minerals). It may sound slightly crazy, but biodynamism seems to work! Come on, let's have a glass of wine and judge for ourselves!

of vines instead of stripping back everything to the bare soil with herbicides. Sometimes they even put in specific plants between the rows, known as 'cover crops', which provide nitrogen and other nutrients in the soil. They might even introduce natural predators to the vineyard to mop up any unwanted insects – ladybirds are employed in this way to get rid of aphids and other small insects. No chemicals means a healthier environment for the workers too.

It all sounds wonderful, but it comes at a price. Organic farming is more labour-intensive, which pushes up the cost of production: expect some organic wines to cost a little more than similar non-organic bottles. And to qualify as organic, there are strict rules and regulations which must be adhered to. The organic grower can't just pick up a chemical spray to help him out of a particularly poor harvest. So when the conditions are terrible – too wet and humid, for example, conditions which can encourage certain diseases – the grape crop suffers and it's just tough luck for the winemaker. That's why organic viticulture works best in dry wine regions that have reliably good weather, and less well in unpredictable, cooler, damper regions.

Today there are many wine producers moving towards organic methods. They recognise that using fewer sprays and fertilisers is good for the land. They might not go all the way and become fully organic, but they only use sprays in emergencies. These winemakers can't register their wines as officially 'organic' but they might let you know their leanings on the back-label text. Generally, the world of wine is moving away from the days when sprays were used widely and frequently, and that's definitely a good thing. Organic – or near-organic – winemakers seem to care more in general about related issues like vineyard workers' health, ecological ethics in the winery, 'green' packaging and recycling, and pollution and how to prevent it, all of which is good news.

Some people think these wines won't give you a hangover – not true, because they are just as alcoholic as any other wines, and too much alcohol will, of course, cause hangovers. But those who worry about the trace residues of chemicals – and any reaction to those – should try to go organic, and if you have a strong reaction to sulphur, which is added in the winery to preserve wine, it helps to know that the regulations permit smaller amounts of sulphur in the production of organic wine.

It gets tricky when you come to look for organic wines in the shops, though. Not all of it is labelled clearly. Look closely at both front and

back labels, and in particular for one of the logos from an organic organisation that will let you know the wine has been passed as organic – in the UK, it is often the Soil Association logo. Alternatively you can ask your wine merchant or shop by mail order or online – good mail-order brochures and websites often make it clear which wines they stock are organic.

And finally, for those who really get into the whole subject of organic wine, don't miss out on 'biodynamic' bottles. Biodynamie is a more extreme version of organic grape growing, where winemakers follow the lunar and planetary cycles to chart when they should work on the vines and harvest. They use ancient treatments like ground-up cow horn silica and homeopathy to work on their land and vines. They are of course fully organic. Sounds batty? The results speak for themselves – vines grown by biodynamic methods seem to be healthier and the wines generally set a high standard. More and more top producers are turning to biodynamie. See Jean-Marc's tip on page 114.

Grower Profile Sergio Mottura

The medieval town of Civitella D'Agliano in central Italy is a very special place. Located where the borders of Lazio, Tuscany and Umbria meet, it's perfectly situated to enjoy the best of these three regions, and is home to a very special winemaker, Sergio Mottura.

Sergio is a boutique producer, specialising in organic production. He's won many international awards. His logo and the symbol of his business is a porcupine, because these delicate animals can only survive and thrive in a truly organic environment – Sergio's vineyards are full of them, and you can spot their quills as you walk through the vines. The secret of his success without chemicals lies with his selection of grape varieties. His theory was that the ancient Etruscans, who it's documented made wine in the region dating back to the 9th century BC, obviously didn't use chemicals, so he re-introduced the ancient Etruscan grape varieties to the area in an effort to make his wine as environmentally friendly and pure as possible. Other producers are now following his lead and embracing the old native vines.

The Mottura estate is spread over 130 hectares (more than 321 acres), nestling between the hills and the clay canyons of Civitella d'Agliano to the west and the fertile plains of the Tiber river valley to the East. Although it's only 100 km from Rome and 160 km from Florence,

Between the villages the land is mostly farmed, and the breathtaking vista is dotted with woods, lakes and streams.

it is an area of unspoilt natural beauty, with the hilltop villages rising out of the landscape like islands in the sea. Between the villages the land is mostly farmed, and the breathtaking vista is dotted with woods, lakes and streams. The stunning backdrop of the Umbrian mountains is a constant, but each month the colours of the landscape change with the maturing vines, swathes of sunflowers, poppies in the hay and the green of tobacco as the growing seasons move through the year. It's an incredibly fertile region and there is always something to wonder at whenever you visit.

Sergio lives amongst his work. His house is in the middle of his vineyards and he can literally walk straight into the vines from his back door. Poggio della Costa, one of his most successful wines, is named after the house, which is surrounded by the Grechetto grapes that make this fabulous wine.

The first thing Sergio does each day is walk through the vines to check their progress. Because they are farmed organically they're more delicate and prone to the effects of the weather. Other growers can compensate for poor climate or pests with chemicals throughout the year, but Sergio's fate is determined by nature. Consequently his yield per hectare is lower, and a bad decision at a crucial time can cost him his whole harvest. The relatively low yields mean the wine is more precious, and consequently some of the wines are slightly more expensive, but he produces something for everyone from the casual drinker to the connoisseur. The best news is that no chemicals means less chance of feeling bad after a night of drinking!

The wine business is a real family affair. One of Sergio's twin sons, Giuseppe, is the winemaker, therefore directly responsible for the process once the grapes leave the fields, and Sebastiano, Sergio's youngest son, has already started learning about cultivation, accompanying his father in the vineyards. Sergio himself can best be described as an elegant gentleman, full of charm. Award-winning Italian chef Gennaro Contaldo, Jamie Oliver's inspiration and owner of top London restaurant Passione, loves Sergio's wine and is impressed by his style and grace that he says represent old Italian values. When they met

SUSY ATKINS' EXPERT TIP

Dinner Party Success
It's often difficult to choose from a large number of wines for a dinner party and sometimes you end up with loads of different bottles on the table. Here's a clever way to organise it: choose an aperitif wine that suits the starter too. For example, a chilled light, dry Italian white, like the Orvieto featured in this chapter, is an elegant and refreshing start to the evening, so plan a starter that goes with it – say, a simple fish or salad dish – and ask your friends to bring their glasses through to the table and carry on with the same wine for the first course. Then make a very definite switch to something richer (a more full-bodied white or a red) to go with the main course, and change the glasses at this stage. Simple stuff, but thinking like this about the wine makes all the difference to the smooth running of your evening.

in England recently, Gennaro was amused that Sergio had even brought a special pair of Italian leather shoes for the rain so that he could always be perfectly turned out.

The precarious nature of organic wine production means the Motturas have had to diversify to maintain a stable income. They have a hotel based in the family's former ancestral seat in the square of Civitella D'Agliano, which is managed by Sergio's partner Alessandra. The name of the hotel, Tana dell'Istrice, means 'the porcupine's lair', underlining the link with the wine and emphasising their use of organic produce. From the hotel windows you get a wonderful snapshot of Italian life, as locals stop to talk, the church bell summons everyone to Mass and the old clock chimes – not quite on time – as a flock of pigeons circle the historic tower or wash in the trickling fountain. The hotel is perfect for wine lovers as it focuses on the whole 'wine experience' from vineyard to table. Guests meet the family, tour the vineyards and the ancient cellars that stretch far beneath the main square, and end each day with a 'wine experience' meal. Alessandra selects local dishes and creates menus that perfectly match each of Sergio's wines.

These tasting dinners are a gastronomic assault on the senses, where guests eat up to seven courses. They are an exploration of local cuisine as well as a lesson in food and wine matching. A lot of the food comes direct from their estate to ensure its organic authenticity – from extra virgin olive oil to salad, fruit, vegetables and even jam that they get the local Trappist monks to make from the estate's own organic crops. The rest comes from trusted local suppliers who rear their own geese or make their own pecorino cheese. This way the family can tell you where everything came from and how it was cultivated.

JOE WADSACK'S EXPERT TIP

Using an Ice Bucket for Fast Results

The temperature that wine should be served at is a real bone of contention for many. In my mind, most reds are served too warm and most whites are served too cold. Some people, including me, think that many reds can be chilled in summer because it tightens them up and makes them more refreshing. Rosé certainly should be chilled. Serious philosophical arguments aside, the most important thing is to know how to chill a bottle correctly, using the most essential piece of wine kit, the ice bucket. It's amazing how few hotels and restaurants know how to prepare an ice bucket properly, so here goes . . . Fill the bucket one third full with ice straight from the freezer, then lay the bottle of wine on top of the cubes. Place under a cold running tap until the ice cubes loosen up enough for the bottle to fall through the cubes to the bottom of the bucket. Turn off the tap. This is pretty much always the ideal amount of water. Now, here is the trade secret . . . add a tablespoon of salt. This will lower the melting point of the water in the bucket from 0 degrees to around minus 10 degrees. Although the ice cubes will melt much quicker, the ice bucket will become far colder. This will chill a warm bottle of wine in less than five minutes. An ice bucket prepared without salt takes more than twice as long, and a bucket with just ice and no water at all, like you get in most hotels these days, can take over twenty minutes!

Sergio serves his idea of the perfect wine with each course and lets the guests decide if they agree with his choices because, as he says, at the end of the day, wine appreciation is all about personal enjoyment – if a wine doesn't suit your palette, that's ok. He explains in his wonderfully romantic Italian accent the qualities of each wine and how they are produced. It is impossible not to be entertained. The evening always begins with a glass (or two) of Sergio's Spumante in the cellar. This is a Champagne-style sparkling wine made from 100% Chardonnay grapes, fermented in bottles stored deep in cellars carved from the Tufo rock under the hotel. The cellars get increasingly colder as you travel deeper underground, and the mist from your breath and the mould on the bottles can give you a distinctly spooky feel, although the family say they have never seen a ghost.

The meal ends with Sergio's most precious wine – Muffo – made from 100% Grechetto. Rare because of its risky production, success cannot be guaranteed. The grapes are grown at low altitude, exposed to the early morning mists from Lake Alviano, and stay on the vine until the misty weather causes 'noble rot' (botrytis cinerea), a special kind of mould which gives the wine its unique taste. (See Jean-Marc's tip on page 270.) This all has to be timed perfectly, as in a matter of hours the grapes can spoil. Only a skilled craftsman can pull this off – the result a unique wine from a truly unique grower.

Grape Variety
Grechetto

Sergio Mottura's Orvieto wine is made from more than one grape variety – it is a blend of four. Grechetto, Procanico, Verdello and Drupeggio may not be as familiar as Chardonnay and Sauvignon Blanc, but they are all traditional Italian white grapes. In fact, the extraordinarily wide range of grapes grown in Italy is considered one of its great strengths, as this ensures many different kinds of wine, each with their own unique flavours and aromas, are made from region to region throughout the country.

In our featured wine, each of the four varieties adds something of its own individual character to the finished product, but the most important grape in this wine is Grechetto, one of Sergio Mottura's favourites. Grechetto has a tangy, crisp, mouth-watering quality, with a fresh floral aroma, juicy citrus fruit and, when young, a hint of pears and bananas. Sometimes there is even a light nutty – some say almondy – note in wines containing Grechetto grapes. It plays an important part in fine aromatic white wines in central Italy. Drink these wines while they are fairly young and vibrant – this is not a variety that needs to age.

Tasting Notes Sergio Mottura Orvieto Classico

Susy Atkins
'This is a lively, refreshing, elegant white wine with clean, tangy flavours of freshly chopped lemon and lime. It's quite subtle – don't expect rich, pungeant aromas or mouth-filling flavours, but enjoy it as a delightful, easy-going aperitif or as a match for simple fish dishes and salads. The finish is dry, tangy and mouth-watering, and there's a subtle hint of creamy ground almonds in there too which adds a little richness.'

Joe Wadsack
'The colour is pale straw with flecks of silver – you know there's something there, it's practically winking at you. The smell has a whiff of freshly baked bread about it. This is because it has been conditioned on "fine lees", the yeast deposits left over after the fermentation. The texture and feel of the wine in the mouth has a creamy density, with a crisp toothsome lick about it that would be the perfect foil to a plate of linguine and clams. Mmm! Go on, you know you want to!'

Jean-Marc Sauboua
'A fascinating white, richly textured yet very open and elegant, supported by a vibrant structure; this is graceful and intense, followed by a long aftertaste of citrus, spices and minerals. Simply fantastic Italian – you can taste the organic side of this wine. It ends on a clean, pure finish, but please drink it well chilled! Drink young when it's at its freshest, and definitely within twelve months.'

Italian whites of today are fresh, zingy and have loads of personality – Sergio Mottura's hand-picked, carefully crafted Orvieto is no exception. It's crisp, clean, refreshing and dry with a subtle hint of truffles, so ideal as an aperitif or with fish dishes. Don't keep it – drink it young and fresh and enjoy it.

Wine Style Guide Light Whites

BESPOKE GROWERS AND ORGANIC PRODUCTION · SERGIO MOTTURA, ITALY

If you like unoaked, dry, aromatic white wines, the good news is there are loads of other similar styles to explore. All the following wines are well worth trying to compare and contrast with the Mottura Orvieto. Served well chilled, they make mouth-watering aperitifs and go well with lighter savoury dishes, especially fish, seafood, salads and creamy pasta sauces.

Still in Italy, you are spoilt for choice, so sample Frascati, Soave, Verdicchio and Pinot Grigio, among others. These are also all unoaked, fresh, light whites. Try to trade up from the cheapest examples, which can taste bland. Just a pound or so more should get you a premium Italian white with a more fruity flavour.

Further afield, do try the wonderfully refreshing and elegant dry Rieslings of Germany. German whites have been out of vogue for some time but the fine Rieslings are a million miles away from old-fashioned Liebfraumilch and there are signs that their popularity is picking up. Riesling has a crisp tanginess, quite naturally low alcohol levels and a delightful apple and lemon flavour. Top examples age beautifully over many years. There is a clean, pure elegance about German Riesling that is hard to beat, especially as an aperitif wine or with fish. If you find you like Riesling from Germany, try one from Austria, or a riper, lime-drenched Australian version.

In France, the mouth-watering bone-dry Sauvignon Blancs made in Sancerre and Pouilly-Fumé in the Loire Valley are seriously classy and subtle, and should appeal to all fans of light, refreshing whites. But they can be fairly expensive, in which case, switch to Sauvignon de Touraine (same grape, same region, smaller price tag). Other light whites can be found in the south and south-west of France, in the form of Vin de Pays des Côtes de Gascogne, an easy-drinking party white that's great value, Bergerac Blanc and the inexpensive, lighter Bordeaux whites, often made with some Sauvignon Blanc too. Also try the aromatic, slightly spicy, unoaked whites of Alsace in north-eastern France.

Outside Europe, and in hotter vineyard areas, the whites tend to be more heavily perfumed and taste richer and riper. One exception is the well-balanced, modern Sauvignon Blanc now emerging from South Africa's vineyards. While you're browsing the South African section, try a Chenin Blanc for a (generally) unoaked, lime-and-guava-flavoured quaffing white, a good all-rounder for parties. Finally, give a New Zealand Sauvignon Blanc a try: you'll get a richer blast of aroma and bags of gooseberry flavour but this is still an unoaked, pure, fruity style of white – like the Mottura Orvieto but with the volume turned up! A fascinating, distinctive style of dry white, Kiwi Sauvignon Blanc is a modern classic that all white-wine lovers should try. See our featured wine in Chapter 9.

How to Get the Best from Your Wine Waiter or Sommelier

Don't be scared of wine waiters! They're supposed to be there to help you make a good choice, not make you quake in your seat. Remember, you are effectively paying them, so make the most of them; they can help stretch your taste and improve your knowledge. Some wine lists seem bafflingly long or short on helpful hints, so don't suffer in silence. Ask the waiter to find a bottle that goes with your dish, or tell him/her what you like to drink and get them to point out something similar. Or request that they find you something brilliant that you've never tried before, but let them know your price bracket! Never be embarrassed about your budget, and stick to it – it's their job to serve you a good wine at the right price; after all, they are often responsible for selecting the wines for the list, so they should be confident in the standard of the complete selection.

The wine waiter should let you try the wine before pouring out a proper glassful for everyone. They should check with you it's the bottle you ordered and that it's chilled to your taste. Give it a good sniff and slurp (time to use those wine-tasting skills). This is your chance to send it back if you think it's faulty. Do just that if the wine seems musty or unpleasantly pongy, or if it's simply rough or completely flat and devoid of flavour and aroma (see page 113 for how to spot if a wine is corked). Don't accept it if you are not happy with it, exactly the same as with sub-standard food. The waiter should quickly bring a replacement bottle, or you can request something different.

In a restaurant, don't forget to try wines by the glass (be clever and find something that goes with each course) and make sure all whites, rosés and sparklers are served fresh and cold. The basic 'house' wines can be good, but they can also be a way of fobbing off naff wine on unknowing diners, so consider moving away from them and up the list a bit.

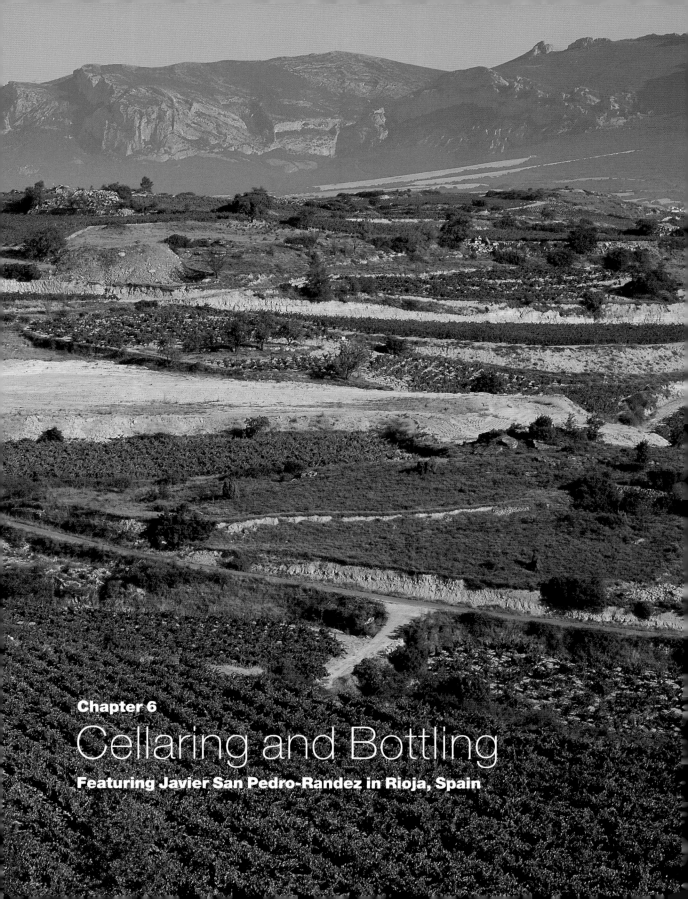

Chapter 6
Cellaring and Bottling
Featuring Javier San Pedro-Randez in Rioja, Spain

Ageing Wines

Most wine is released ready to drink – indeed, the vast majority of bottles are lapped up within a couple of days of leaving the shop! Gone are the days when much wine was made to be cellared for years and enjoyed when it was at its best, perhaps a very long time after buying.

But you can still find these wines. If you want to buy wine to 'lay down' – this doesn't have to be in a cellar but do store bottles on their sides somewhere cool and dark (see page 42 on how to store wine) – then look for young, premium clarets, vintage port, fine dessert wines, or any very intense and tough red such as top Californian Cabernet Sauvignon, Italian Barolo or Aussie Shiraz. There are some white wines that repay ageing – white Burgundy, some top Loire Chenin Blancs and the best German Rieslings are good examples. Expensive vintage Champagne is often too sharp and edgy when young, and needs eight or ten years to be at its best. All these wines have concentrated flavours, rich tannins and/or firm acidity – these factors all mellow and soften over time but keep the wines fresh while the softening happens.

Otherwise, drink wines up soon after you buy them. This is especially important for fragile, light wines that will grow tired and fruitless after a short time – we've already seen that rosé (Chapter 4) needs to be cracked open quickly, but so do tangy, crisp, light and simple whites like Italian Frascati, Soave and Orvieto, dry and pale sherries, inexpensive Sauvignon Blanc, cheap fizz and basic jammy reds.

JOE WADSACK'S EXPERT TIP

Dealing with Wine Stains
A bit of red wine on the carpet is a sign of a good party, but it doesn't make you feel better when you see the stain the next morning though, does it? Well, the trick is to be prepared for it. When I have a party, I put a carpet foam cleaner behind the curtain in every room! Maybe that's overkill, but the two essentials to bear in mind are that time is of the essence, and that lifting the stain is the best way to stop it fixing permanently. If you don't have a foam upholstery cleaner, shaving foam squirted directly into the pile, or even a soda siphon, does a remarkably good job. The old adage that white wine gets red wine stains out is nothing more than a wives' tale – white wine can stain too!

Water does pretty well. Another trick often mentioned is the use of salt on a wine stain – it actually does quite a good job of decolourising red wine stains but it tends to fix it at the same time, so don't do this to white fabrics!

Understanding the Ageing of Rioja

Rioja is different in a crucial way. Although it needs some age, it's matured at the winery, ready for drinking when it hits the shops. The Spanish age the wine in oak barrels and, after bottling it, they keep it in their cellars for even longer, until it's ideally mellow, soft and delicious. Anyone buying red Rioja should not hang on to it – the winery has done the ageing process for you, so get on and enjoy it!

Traditional Rioja is generally aged in American (and occasionally French) oak barrels. But some modern Riojas are made without any barrel ageing for an easy-drinking, fruity style of red. Our featured wine is just like this – made with 100% Tempranillo grape but not oak aged, and released when young for a more modern, fresh, lively style of wine. These reds often say 'sin crianza' on the label, which means 'without wood'. Another word to look out for is 'joven', which means 'young'.

If a red Rioja says 'crianza' on the label, it means it has been aged at the 'bodega' – the Spanish name for a winery – for at least two years, and for one of these years the wine was in oak cask. These wines start to show a more woody, aromatic and spicy note, and they are likely to be more full-bodied, but they will not be as mellow and soft as a traditional older Rioja.

To get that character, choose a wine that says 'reserva' on the label – Rioja reservas have spent at least three years at the winery, with one in cask. The most venerable and elderly Riojas are labelled 'gran reserva'. These prized bottles are made only in the best years and they rest in the bodega for at least five years after being made, with at least two years in oak casks. Many believe gran reserva Rioja to be among the best red wine in the world, although lovers of the New World style of fruit-forward, fresh and juicy red might find them too mellow and prefer a younger wine. Old reds tend to taste less of fresh fruits and chewy tannins, and become more leathery, spicy, even earthy in flavour with a smoother, softer texture.

As always in wine, it's up to you to decide if you like older or younger styles. A good guide is to think about when you would want to drink the wine. Young, fruity, soft reds are fine on their own or with a wide range of simple savoury food, while young powerful, chewy, tannic reds need rich protein such as rare steak or hard cheese to tame them and soften them in the mouth and are no fun on their own. Older, rounded reds are fabulous with rich roast meats, game and mature cheeses. There's more about decanting tough red wines and the effects of aerating a wine in Joe's expert tip on page 70.

Bottling – Corks or Screw Caps

In the Rioja region of Spain, it is mandatory to use natural cork to stopper the bottles, but in other parts of the winemaking globe the use of plastic stoppers and screw caps is now quite common. So what are the pros and cons of each method and what should you look out for?

This issue is being hotly debated by wine professionals around the world – it really is the issue of the moment! Join the debate by tasting wines with natural corks, plastic stoppers and screw caps, comparing them for freshness, ageing ability and ease of use. Here are some of the factors to look out for:

Natural cork: Surveys show that most consumers still prefer natural cork and think of it as the most classy and appealing way to package wine. Some of the romance of wine is about popping out a natural cork, they argue, and it just isn't the same with plastic or screw caps. But there is a worryingly high incidence of cork taint out there – this happens when a bad cork infects the wine with a mouldy, musty smell and flavour. Some experts reckon one in twenty bottles at least is tainted. In acute cases, this mustiness is easily spotted, but in smaller doses, cork taint merely flattens the fresh fruit character of the wine, making it seem dull. If you think you have a corked wine, either in a restaurant or bought from the shop, always take it back and demand a replacement. Cork producers are now working hard to eradicate taint and some seem close to doing so. Wines bottled under natural cork do generally age well and many believe this is because cork allows for a minute exchange of air inside the bottle, and therefore a gradual and tiny amount of oxidation.

Plastic stoppers: These prevent cork taint and some are made to look like natural cork, but they are notoriously difficult to get off the corkscrew and often hard to stick back in an unfinished bottle between servings. What's more, we simply don't know how well wine ages under plastic yet.

JEAN-MARC SAUBOUA'S EXPERT TIP

Cork Taint
My biggest enemy as a winemaker is 2,4,6-Trichloroanisole . . . no, it's not an alien creature but the technical name for corked wine. A contaminated cork causes corked wine, giving a mouldy or musty-like aroma. This fault is sometimes very obvious but a little cork taint may just dull the wine. A mildly corked wine might well be less fruity than you remember and only have a slight musty aroma, it does not mean it will be undrinkable. Incidentally, having a piece of cork floating in your wine glass has nothing to do with a cork-tainted wine! But please don't be a cork snob: some modern alternatives lack cork's cachet, but they can give you a guaranteed fresher wine. Plastic corks are now common and are sometimes used by high-quality producers to preserve the fruit in wine. A screw top is another great option and snobbery is all that prevents its widespread use!

Screw caps: Time was when only cheap plonk came with a screw cap. Now, more and more premium wine is bottled this way, with the Australians and New Zealanders leading the way, although many progressive Europeans are now converts too. These modern producers don't have to worry about cork taint, and they like the convenient way you can get into and reseal your bottles with a screw cap. It has been argued that the lightest, crispest, most aromatic dry white wines are the best candidates for screw caps, as these seem to show up cork taint more easily than other wines; that's why you often see Riesling and Sauvignon Blanc with screw caps. Big powerful reds show taint much less, and as these are the types of wine that age well under very slightly permeable corks, some winemakers use screw caps for whites and corks for reds. Some say that it's no good using completely airtight screw caps for wines that are meant to be aged for a long time – there is absolutely no exchange of air, which is needed if the wine is to evolve slowly.

Ultimately, we predict that cork will have to get its act together if screw-cap machines aren't going to take over in the majority of wineries. But there are signs that cork taint is being tackled at last, and let's hope in the next few years that finally happens. At the moment, the number of times a musty wine crops up in a tasting is still unacceptably high. After all, you'd change your milkman if he delivered a pint that tasted musty and horrible simply because of its old-fashioned packaging, wouldn't you?

Grower Profile
Javier San Pedro-Randez

Rioja has long enjoyed enormous fame as Spain's foremost red wine-producing region. The British in particular adore the soft, mellow, but concentrated strawberry flavours of the famed aged red Rioja, and now many are being won over to the new wave of unoaked modern styles emerging.

It's a region impregnated with wine culture, according to Javier San Pedro-Randez, the ebullient and charismatic owner of the San Pedro winery. 'Centuries before the name Rioja appeared, wine was already the basis of this region's wealth,' he explains. 'Celebrations, festivities, customs, traditions and even the language all reveal many references to vines and wines. There's no other Spanish region with such a strong wine heritage as Rioja.' Javier believes the whole culture of the place has been developed around the winemaker's calendar.

He should know! Not only is he the owner of San Pedro, but Javier is also mayor of the town of Laguardia, in the heart of the Rioja wine-producing region. Rioja is in the Ebro river valley in the central-northern part of Spain, far away from the tourist resorts of the costas. At its north it borders the Sierra Cantabria mountain range, and there, in the foothills, lies Laguardia, a picturesque, medieval walled town. Laguardia occupies a hilltop position, a permanent reminder of its days as a fortress town, as its name implies, guarding the area from enemies, nestling within the stunning scenery and vast vineyards of the region.

Javier is fiercely proud of this part of Spain. 'Working in Rioja and with Rioja's wines means everything to me – it's my life,' he says. 'I was born here, I grew up and became a wine professional here, and I've always been surrounded by Rioja's vineyards and wineries.'

He comes from a family with a long tradition of winemaking. When he was a child, he accompanied his grandfather, also a wine producer, to the vineyards and to work in the winery. 'Little by little, some of his wisdom was learned!' he recalls. Later, the young Javier trained alongside his father at the family winery, which made mass-produced, inexpensive wines. He became involved with his father's business at the tender age of fourteen and, although his father had gained a good reputation for bulk wine, Javier grew up determined to produce top-quality labels. In 1987, while still in his twenties, he founded Bodegas San Pedro.

Rioja is made up of three zones – Rioja Alta, Rioja Baja and Rioja Alavesa. San Pedro is located in Rioja Alavesa, to the north of the region. Many believe that the red wines made from fruit grown here in yellow calcareous soils are the most delicately scented and elegant of all. It is widely planted with the Tempranillo variety, the great traditional red grape of Rioja, which enjoys the relatively cool climate and chalky-clay soils. San Pedro today owns 90 hectares of vines, mainly Tempranillo, with a little Garnacha. Some of the vineyards are those Javier and his brother inherited from their family at the beginning of 2000.

The style of the wines from San Pedro is very personal, reflecting the strong preferences of Javier. They tend to be concentrated, with ripe fruit and good complexity. He says the most important factor is grace – he positively dislikes any aggressive or chewy tannins in his wines! 'When I'm making a red, I always aim for a wine with elegance and personality,' he says. 'The wine should be a pile of sensations – I hope it has great aroma, presence and flavours, something for all the senses.'

He loves matching Rioja with food – indeed, anyone on a visit to the region should spend some time in the local tapas bars, experimenting with a wide range of the little dishes served there, and pairing them with Rioja's wines, red, white and rosé. Javier lets us in on the latest local gastronomic trends: 'Nowadays in Laguardia, the cooks are

deliberately turning back towards traditional Spanish flavours. So we see potatoes with *chorizo* – a highly seasoned pork sausage – or *pochas*, which are white cooked beans, or veal chops, all of which go well with our red wines.' His favourite dish, he declares, is 'a good ox chop', washed down with a glass of crianza wine – fairly young, oaky red Rioja. 'The tannins combine perfectly with the meat,' he says.

San Pedro is seen as a role model for new small wineries in the area and Javier is clearly excited about the future in Rioja: 'The region has experienced important changes. Our young winemakers have adapted themselves well to new trends, always trying to keep quality in the wines. Many of them have been quite pioneering, while keeping the traditions in vineyards and wineries as a basis.'

It's certainly true that the region has managed to evolve cleverly in the modern era, producing traditional wines from Tempranillo, aged in classic American oak for many years, while experimenting with different styles of wine – more fruit-driven, less oaky and including different grape varieties. Now there is not one single style of Rioja, but many to choose from. Traditionalists won't be disappointed as the crianzas, reservas and gran reservas are still there, but those who were weaned on the fruit-driven, fresh styles of the New World will love new-wave red Rioja, like our featured wine.

Javier has recently launched two white wines, made from the Spanish grape Viura. One is barrel-fermented, one is not. 'It was a great experiment for me because I had never made this kind of wine before, and we've had to expand the winery in order to make space for it.' Somehow, it seems unlikely that the youthful, dynamic owner of San Pedro, aka Mayor of Laguardia, will ever stop looking for new ways to keep busy!

SUSY ATKINS' EXPERT TIP

Getting the Best from Your Glass
Go easy on the washing up! No, that isn't a suggestion that you leave everything till the morning, but a serious point about washing-up liquid, which can do terrible things to wine, especially sparkling wine. Leftover detergent on a glass can change the flavour of the next wine you pour into it, so make sure you rinse glasses very thoroughly after cleaning them. With Champagne glasses, avoid using detergent for cleaning altogether – the slightest hint of soap will kill bubbles dead next time you crack open the fizz. Now you know why you sometimes get a flat glassful while your friend gets lots of froth from the same bottle of fizz – you had the soapier glass! Champagne and sparkling-wine glasses should just be rinsed well under a very hot tap and then use a linen tea towel to rub them dry and shiny, making sure you get any lipstick off. Store glasses upside-down to stop dust getting into them, and away from the cooker, where a greasy film can form on them. Wherever you store them, always look at your glasses and give them a quick dust and shine-up before using, especially if you've bought a very good bottle of wine and want to show it off to perfection.

Grape Variety
Tempranillo

This is Spain's greatest grape, and the one that makes many of its top reds. Tempranillo has been described as 'Spain's answer to Cabernet Sauvignon' and it has got some similarities to the more famous French variety, giving deeply coloured, long-lived reds with lots of rich fruit and concentration. Tempranillo, though, is often used to make plenty of mellow, soft, aged reds in Rioja and the rest of Spain, rather than predominantly powerfully tannic ones. It also has a more red-berry flavour – think strawberries rather than Cabernet's cassis and blackcurrant. It has quite low acidity and sometimes conjures up nuances of fresh tobacco and leather, making red wines that are especially good with rich lamb dishes, garlicky roast vegetables and mature cheeses.

The name 'Tempranillo' refers to the Spanish word for 'early', and this grape certainly does ripen early. It can thrive in both cool and warmer spots, and is grown widely across central and northern Spain. The best places for it are Rioja (where it's often blended with Garnacha and Mazuelo grapes and sometimes with Cabernet) and Ribera del Duero, where it is called Tinto Fino. Tempranillo goes under several other names – it's known as Cencibel in Valdepeñas, and in the Penedes region it's exotically named Ull de Llebre.

Despite Tempranillo's great success in several Spanish wine regions, it isn't seen widely overseas. That said, the Argentinians are enjoying some success with the grape, and in Portugal it is grown – under the name Tinta Roriz – as one of the varieties for port and for table wines – under yet another name, Tinta Aragonez.

Tasting Notes San Pedro Rioja

Susy Atkins

'A modern take on red Rioja, with blackcurrant, blackberry and plum flavours, even a hint of red cherry. A bright, lively wine, and although it's not oaky, it does have the smooth, rounded texture I expect from this region. It should be a versatile match for all sorts of red meat dishes, but especially lamb and rich pasta bakes like lasagne.'

Joe Wadsack

'It smells of a baked cherry pie, with a savoury aroma of roasted nuts. Very festive. The texture is very smooth with a plummy, liquoricey flavour and a moreish tangy finish. I bet this would work a treat with a roast ham at Christmas or with a slice of game pie.'

Jean-Marc Sauboua

'Seductive Rioja, racy yet thick, full of ripe fruit and supple tannins. A mouthful of pleasure from start to finish, bursting with blackberries and chocolate notes. Medium bodied with a soft palate and a silky finish. A real Spanish gem, classic and enjoyable. Drink now or keep for up to three years.'

Rioja imported to the UK is mostly barrel-aged (oaked) to add weight, complexity and subtle vanilla flavours. By contrast, the San Pedro has never seen the inside of a barrel so the fruit really is able to speak for itself. You should experience juicy, black-cherry flavours. This wine is delicious with food.

Our featured example of red Rioja is mellow, smooth and fruity. If you like it, do try other reds made from Tempranillo to discover the range of styles from just one grape variety. Try other red Riojas (these may be blends of Tempranillo with Garnacha/Grenache and other grape varieties) and note how much these vary according to age – no oak, crianza, reserva and gran reserva. Some will taste chunkier, oakier and more tannic than our wine; others will be in the same fruit-driven modern style. Which do you like best?

Also try Tempranillo wines from other parts of Spain – remember, it may be called a different name in a different region. The most important area for this grape, outside Rioja, is Ribera del Duero, where, as Tinto Fino, it is capable of making very impressive, serious and expensive Spanish reds. Many people think the wines of the Vega Sicilia and Pesquera wineries in Ribera del Duero show Spain at its very best – but you may need to take out a bank loan to afford them! More down-to-earth and widely available are the juicy, ripe reds of Valdepeñas in the centre of the country, where Tempranillo is called Cencibel.

Taste other Spanish reds for comparison, especially Garnachas, then head north-east across the border and try out south-western French reds, especially Cabernet Sauvignon (for more on this, see page 80). If Tempranillo is really 'Spain's answer to Cabernet', then how do these grapes compare, in your view?

If you like the richer, more powerful styles of Rioja, then do try other 'big' reds. Barolo and Barbaresco, from Piedmont in northern Italy, are classics. Made from the Nebbiolo grape growing in the fog-laden hills of the region, these wines taste and smell savoury, floral and blackberryish all at once. The best are huge and concentrated, yet strangely elegant and well balanced, and they age beautifully.

Try the richer Shirazes from Australia for satisfyingly robust, intense red wines packed with loads of brambly, blackcurrant fruit and a touch of pepper, or go for one of the massive Syrahs (it's the same grape as Shiraz but under a different name) from France's northern Rhône – Côte-Rôtie would be a brilliant buy. Other big reds include the very top Zinfandels and Cabernet Sauvignons of California, the oakier, more serious Merlots from anywhere, and a lot of the premium South African reds, or try a rare but interesting red made from the Tannat grape in Uruguay.

If, however, it was the juicy fruit and softer roundness of our Rioja you particularly enjoyed, then mellow out with some smoother, more easy-going reds. Try Pinot Noir, especially from Burgundy and New Zealand, for silky raspberry-strawberry flavours, and choose more approachable versions of Shiraz/Syrah by picking an inexpensive Cabernet–Shiraz blend from Australia and a simpler Côtes-du-Rhône from France. Or head off into Merlot territory for lots of very fruity plummy flavours. You'll find the best Merlots in France, especially in Bordeaux, or try a bright modern Bulgarian example for good value, or one from America's Washington State, or a New Zealand Merlot from the Hawke's Bay region on the North Island.

CELLARING AND BOTTLING JAVIER SAN PEDRO-RANDEZ, SPAIN

How to Return Faulty Wine: Your Rights

It can be pretty unnerving when you want to return a faulty bottle of wine, so it pays to know your consumer rights before confronting a shop assistant. Here they are.

The Sale of Goods Act 1979 says that wines must: fit any description given to them (on the label, etc.); be of satisfactory quality, i.e. free from defects (this would include cork taint, see page 146); and correspond with any sample you ordered – therefore if you ordered a bottle of wine on the basis of a sample, the wine should taste very similar. If your wine doesn't measure up to these criteria, then it is up to the retailer to sort out the problem – i.e. offer a refund or exchange. So don't suffer in silence – take faulty wines back to the shop, but do make sure you haven't drained the bottle first! A taste or two should be all it takes for you to assess any faults.

In a restaurant, the wine should correspond to the description on the menu and should not be corked or oxidised (see page 109) – otherwise, do not continue drinking it, complain immediately and ask for something else. If the problem is not solved (i.e. a replacement bottle found), then you can deduct the cost of the faulty wine from the bill. Alternatively, pay 'under protest', by writing the words on the back of the cheque, for example, and you can then claim compensation later. If the wine is just not to your taste then the restaurant is under no obligation to replace it. Sorry!

The Rest of the 'Old' Wine World

France, Italy and Spain got a big look-in in the previous pages, so here's a run-down of other countries in Europe that also make wine. Some of them are deeply important to our wine-drinking culture, others have an interesting history of winemaking, and one or two are up-and-coming sources of wine, so well worth keeping an eye on. It always pays to try a wide variety of wine, so do try bottles from far-flung corners of the Old World.

Germany

German wine seems to be coming back into vogue after years when we pigeon holed it as bland, boring and cheap, with names that were impossible to pronounce. But who cares about fashion? If you picked carefully, there were always some great – truly great – German wines out there to be enjoyed. The key was to avoid the obvious. Inexpensive, mass-marketed German white wines (the Liebfraumilches, Hocks and Niersteiners) are generally a bland lot, and it only took a sip of vibrantly fruity, ripe Australian whites to wake us up to the fact and push German wine out of fashion. However, fine German whites, mostly made from the superior Riesling grape, are among the most delightful and refreshing in the world. Expect a tangy, light, appley mouthful with crisp acidity and an appealing floral aroma. Choose a wine labelled Riesling (whether dry, medium or sweet) from Germany and you are well on your way to discovering how appealing the country's best bottles are. Germany now lags well behind France, Italy and Spain (not to mention Australia and the US) in sales to the UK, but the tide is turning as people move away from heavy hot-climate wines and look for more subtlety and finesse, the sort of style provided by delicate wines from cooler vineyards. As well as Riesling, look out for Grauburgunder (aka Pinot Gris or Grigio), Weissburgunder (Pinot Blanc), and reds made from Spätburgunder (Pinot Noir) and Dornfelder. And check out the new wave of modern bottles with easier labels and straightforward brand names – at last!

Portugal

Portuguese wine is about so much more than port, although the fortified wines of the staggeringly beautiful Douro Valley are rightly famous. If you like port, be sure to try the unfortified red wines now also coming from the Douro Valley – made with a blend of port grapes, they are typically concentrated, ripe and complex. Serious stuff, but sometimes pricey. For less money you can get good-value, fruity, everyday reds and whites from the newly modernised Ribatejo, Estremadura and Alentejo regions further south. Some of these come from efficient, fairly high-tech co-operative wineries which have got their act together recently and are making the most of the host of local vines, as well as some familiar grapes like Chardonnay and Cabernet. Some of the powerful red wines from the Dão and Bairrada regions are impressive; others are too tannic and old-fashioned. Vinho Verde is patchy too – although we remember enjoying it in the 1980s, somehow the tart acidity and dodgy sweetness tastes old-fashioned these days. Still, with those up-and-coming areas further south and the new Douro reds, Portugal has plenty of other cards to play.

Austria

Austria's wines are a well-kept secret – although they are hugely popular among those 'in the know' and connoisseurs, they should get more credit in general. The top whites are excellent, especially the spine-tingling dry Rieslings, those made from Grüner Veltliner (Austria's signature grape, which usually makes dry whites tasting of zesty grapefruit and white pepper) and luscious, top-notch dessert wines. Try bottles from the Wachau region for the best dry whites, and those from Burgenland for impressive 'sweeties'. Ripe, surprisingly chunky reds can be found too, but you may have to go to Austria to find them. We hope Austrian wine will reach a wider audience – it definitely deserves to. Expect more in the future. Most of the wine comes from the south of the country, where some promising reds and sparkling wines seem to be the pick of the crop. As with so many emerging wine regions, talented winemakers from around the world are flying in to grab a share of the action, and their words of wisdom are helping improve quality no end.

THE REST OF THE 'OLD' WINE WORLD

Bulgaria

It's disappointing to see Bulgaria reduced to 'also-ran' status when the ripe, easy-drinking, medium-bodied reds were so popular ten or fifteen years ago. But major problems started to show (revolving around vineyard ownership, run-down wineries and a general lack of investment) after the Communist era was over – it's a muddle that has yet to be sorted out. Let's hope Bulgaria eventually bounces back. Meanwhile, among some patchy quality over all, there are still a few bargains to be found on supermarket shelves, mainly reds made from Cabernet Sauvignon, Merlot, and local grapes Mavrud and Melnik.

Hungary

It's definitely worth tracking down some Hungarian wine, especially if you are on a budget. Inexpensive reds and whites have proved surprisingly good. Avoid the rough Bull's Blood and instead plump for the dry white wines made from spicy Irsai Oliver, Riesling and Furmint. Above all, make sure you don't miss the fabulous dessert wine Tokaji (Furmint is its main grape variety), fresh but honeyed, luscious and brilliant with many puddings and cakes, but especially chocolate. A classic.

Greece

The country that made so much wine in ancient times is finally starting to impress in the modern era with some pleasing aromatic, rich whites and intensely flavoured reds, made from international grape varieties as well as local Greek ones. Banish your memories of nasty taverna wines on holiday – these are quite different from retsina, which is made with added pine resin for a woody flavour, and taste much more like 'normal', premium quality table wine. Wrap your tongue around grape varieties that include Roditis, Moscophilero and Assyrtico (whites), and Aghiorghitiko, Mavrodaphne and Xinomavro (reds).

England

Yep, English wines are definitely worth a try. That's English wines, not British wines. British wine is made from imported grape juice; English wines are made from English grapes grown in the English vineyards! The best bets are the aromatic, light whites – some are beautifully elegant, with an aroma of fresh spring flowers, and appley/citrus flavours. Think Loire Sauvignon Blanc and German Riesling and you're in the general style-area. English fizz can be exciting too – our cool climate means we can make crisp, refreshing sparkling wine. Fine reds are less common – one or two are ripe and rich enough, but they tend to be expensive.

The New World

In the 1970s, Australian wine was a national (and international) joke – even featuring in Monty Python sketches, the first vines were only just being planted among the sheep in Marlborough. New Zealand and South African wine was typically rough fortified plonk. On the British high street, the shops were stuffed largely with European bottles.

Fast forward to the 21st century and Australia is the number one choice for wine drinkers in the UK. Oz and the other 'New World' wine countries, have wiped plenty of traditional 'Old World' bottles off the shelves. Here's an amazing fact: nearly one in every four bottles of wine sold in wine shops comes from Down Under, around one in six is Californian, and one in ten is South African. If you'd told us that back in 1975, we'd never have believed it possible.

So how has the so-called 'New World' of wine done it? For one, it has a new generation of enthusiastic, dynamic, forward-thinking winemakers. These guys (and girls) are carefully trained in how to make wine, and they have usually travelled to the European wine regions to pick up tips (and perhaps, learn from others' mistakes!). They often work in new, state-of-the-art wineries, making it their business to stay ahead of the game, following all the latest developments in the vineyard and high-tech new discoveries for the winery.

A warm, reliable climate is another reason – many of the New World wine regions have consistently fine summers, with plenty of hot sunshine to ensure tasty wine, year after year, almost effortlessly.

It's also easier for the customer to choose and discriminate among these wines: a typical old-fashioned label from France, Germany or Italy can baffle most of us – naming places instead of grape varieties, perhaps using difficult Gothic script and confusing terms so we don't really know what to expect from the wine inside the bottle. In the New World, wines are labelled more simply.

A typical New Zealand bottle, for example, might say Villa Maria (winery name), Sauvignon Blanc (grape variety), 2005 (year), Marlborough (region). Bingo – it does exactly what it says on the label!

Interestingly, they often use the same grape varieties – Chardonnay, Cabernet Sauvignon, Merlot, Pinot Noir and Shiraz (aka Syrah in France) have thrived all around the world. It has led to some accusations that New World wines tend to be a bit bland and uniform – they all taste the same, say some critics, with ripe, bright, upfront fruity flavours, loads of oak, but a lack of real character and complexity. This is true of the inexpensive labels and some of the big, ubiquitous New World brands.

However, the best New World winemakers are increasingly making wines that show regional character and style, toning down the oak and sweet jamminess to come up with more individual, distinctive flavours. They are using cooler-climate fruit for a fresh, crisper, more elegant kind of wine, and employing a wider range of grapes for premium wines – look out for Chilean Carmenère, Australian Riesling, South African Pinotage and Californian Zinfandel, for starters.

There's no reason to get bored with New World wines if you ring the changes regularly and try plenty of different styles. Here we introduce the six most important New World wine lands – Australia, South Africa, New Zealand, California, Chile and Argentina. Learn the extraordinary story of wine in each country and why they are so successful – which types of wine and which grapes are essential to try from every region, and what the pioneering winemakers have to say about the New World revolution in wine, one of the great success stories of our time. In each chapter, as before, we have selected a signature bottle of wine to base our tastings on, and profiled the fascinating grower who produced it. Let the journey continue …

Chapter 7
Australia
Featuring De Bortoli in the Yarra Valley

It might surprise you to know that the Australian wine industry is as old as the modern settlement of Australia itself. Vines were transported with the First Fleet in 1788, although these particular vines didn't prove to be very successful. Then a shipment of vines brought from France by a Scot, James Busby, the grandfather of Australian vine growing, transformed the continent's fortunes. He transported four hundred vine cuttings to find out which were suited to the extreme and varied climates. He's particularly noted for discovering the potential for Shiraz (see page 189) and Verdelho, a white port grape that's still grown successfully across the continent.

By the mid-1820s, Australian wine production had reached around 90 tonnes, much of which was already being shipped to Britain. Australian wines began to win medals at European wine fairs in Brussels and Paris. The rest, as they say, is history, and British drinkers have voted with their wallets: Australian wine now outsells French wine in the UK, something that no industry analyst would have predicted ten years ago. Australia is firmly on the wine map!

When the Australians first began to target the UK, they concentrated not on where the wine was from but which grapes it was made of – their labelling this way made the wine more accessible than the French system. Suddenly the grape variety was king. Chardonnay began to become a household name and people didn't need a degree in geography to select a bottle. No chateaux, no history, just delicious wine.

Australia's size and diverse climate mean that if you can produce a wine in Europe, there is almost certainly a place, discovered or not, somewhere on the continent where you could produce a similar style. Significantly, Australia isn't bound by the same laws as Europe, telling the winemakers what they are allowed to plant where, how much they can produce and so on: everybody is free to experiment as much as they like. Almost every grape variety in the world is available somewhere in Oz, and every style too. World-class sparkling wine is made in the cooler regions, like Southern Victoria and Tasmania,

JEAN-MARC SAUBOUA'S EXPERT TIP

The Importance of Soil
Have you ever noticed that vines are nearly always planted on poor soil? Look at where the wines come from, Châteauneuf-du-Pape – grown in pebbles; St-Emilion – pure solid limestone; Champagne – 100% chalk. In Italy, many vineyards are on terraces or steep hillsides; the fields with good soil are used for cereals. Let me explain why. Vines need to suffer to yield a small amount of grapes with the concentrated and complex flavours needed to make great wine. If the vines have too easy a life, with lots of water and rich soil, they will make an abundant quantity of average fruit and quite possibly uninteresting wines. So, you'll say, what about Southern Hemisphere wines? Well, although some are planted in deep, rich soil, they often struggle with the heat and the lack of water – this also makes them stressed and produces grapes for fine wine. As they say, no pain no gain!

while the torturously hot regions, Rutherglen and Griffith, for example, make top-quality fortified wines that are indistinguishable from top-quality port and sherry. This is not at all surprising, because Australia produced almost nothing but fortified wine for nearly a century, before the advent of refrigeration and modern winemaking innovations transformed their methods.

The huge commercial success of Australian wine was based on full-flavoured Chardonnay and Cabernet Sauvignon during the '80s and '90s, but these have now been overtaken in the fashion stakes by Shiraz, Sauvignon Blanc, Viognier, and the two Australian specialities, Semillon and Riesling. Currently, Italian grape varieties are being produced that will soon be able to challenge Italian wines for quality. The latest craze is the lesser-known Bordeaux variety Petit Verdot, which delivers reliable, profoundly dark, blueberry-infused reds in areas too hot for other varieties. In fact, the key to buying Australian wine is to recognise which areas are best at producing which styles and varieties of wine. Here's a quick run-down of what Australia does where:

Western Australia is a huge state but produces a minuscule amount of wine compared to the other regions. However, it's home to some of the very finest wines and most famous names in the Australian wine industry. Margaret River is where it's at – no other region in Oz has drawn so many parallels with Bordeaux. It's protected from the ocean breezes by pine forests, the vines are planted on an ancient sand bank by the sea and the surf's fantastic – factors all shared with Bordeaux, including the surf! Wineries like Cullen, Leeuwin Estate and Cape Mentelle are among the top ten producers of Australian Chardonnay and Cabernet Sauvignon every year.

South Australia, to quote a famous Australian wine expert, is, and always will be, the womb of the Australian wine industry. It grows most of the grapes, makes most of the wine and is the

JOE WADSACK'S EXPERT TIP

Warming Wine
In winter or at Christmas, there's nothing more frustrating than to reach for a bottle of red wine to go with dinner and find that it's as cold as ice. What can you do? Simply create an ice bucket in reverse. Fill a kitchen sink half full with warm, not boiling-hot, water. Stand the bottle up in the water and feel the bottle every thirty seconds or so. Be careful not to leave it in too long, as the warming process happens rather quickly. This is also the only reason that I can think for having a wine thermometer, as it is so difficult to judge the temperature of the contents through the thick glass. Don't ever leave wine in front of a fire or on the Aga top, because glass is a very efficient heat store. What often happens is that one side of the bottle gets so hot that some of the more delicate flavours and aromas evaporate out, while the other side of the bottle remains very cold. You certainly wouldn't be aware that the wine is damaged, but it would spoil the taste. So, the moral of the story here is to take care!

state where most of the large wine corporations are based. However, there are many tiny enclaves of greatness, far removed from the oceans of reliable but anonymous wine that this region is most famous for. In the hills of the Barossa Valley are vineyards of legendary standing, like Henschke and Rockford. In the Eden Valley, just over the rise to the East are the world-class Riesling vineyards of Yalumba and Penfolds. South of the Barossa is one of the most exciting and coldest regions in Australia, Adelaide Hills, where truly great Pinot Noir, Chardonnay and Sauvignon is being produced by the likes of Nepenthe, Petaluma, and Shaw & Smith.

There are three other regions that must be mentioned – the high altitude Clare Valley to the north, that produces arguably the best non-European Riesling in the world; McLaren Vale, half an hour south of Adelaide, that produces the darkest, richest Shiraz; and way south, Coonawarra, where some of world's finest Cabernet Sauvignon continues to be made by the likes of Penley Petaluma and Katnook Estate.

Victoria is now a hotbed of exciting innovation, although it was the major production centre for the Australian industry a 100 years ago, before disease wiped out the vineyards. It's a region known for its enormous diversity, from the hot, arid vineyards of Milawa, to the snow-capped, alpine climate of Mansfield. This is the home of the wine pioneer, where many small players have chosen to produce small quantities of stellar-quality wine. The most historically famous wine region in Victoria is Rutherglen, where the otherworldly 'Rutherglen Stickies' come from. Usually made from Muscat or Tokay, these wines are considered by many to be the most unctuous, sweet, exotic dessert wines in the world. They are fortified wines, made like port, and in some cases they are aged for approaching a hundred years, a priceless legacy from the time when these were the only type of wines that Australia was able to make.

To the west, some of the finest reds are made by the likes of the Taltarni, Dalwhinnie and Balgownie Estates. Some of Australia's most successful attempts at reproducing the brilliance of the northern Rhône Syrahs come from this state, most notably from Great Western, Moonambel, Heathcote, Macedon and certain parts of the Yarra Valley. The future of red and white Burgundy styles in Australia is in some of Victoria's coolest regions – Yarra Valley, Mornington Peninsular, Geelong and Beechworth. These areas produce startling quality Pinot Noir and Chardonnay, that will one day fetch as much per bottle as the great wines of France.

An emerging region is the now fashionable state of Tasmania, a fantastic source of sparkling wine. Some of the best examples are almost indistinguishable from top-quality vintage French fizz, namely Clover Hill, Jansz and Pirie.

The region that put Australia firmly on the map is the Hunter Valley, partly due to the efforts of local character Len Evans, who was awarded an OBE for his services to the wine industry in 1982. Although the Hunter Valley continues to be very important, and still makes elegant, very long-lived dry Semillon whites and full-bodied gunpowder Shiraz reds, it's the emergence of regions like Mudgee and Orange that looks set to secure the future for this state in the wine history books. Mudgee produces wonderfully silky Cabernet and Shiraz fruit, while the very high altitude and extremes of temperature in Orange have enabled growers to produce excellent Pinot Noir and Merlot.

The pioneering spirit of the Australian wine industry has never been so strong, but it is the small to medium-sized companies who are taking most of the risks, rather than the larger corporate branch. This is their chance to prove how diverse Australian wine can be.

Grower Profile De Bortoli

There's a vanguard of independent, quality-driven wine companies that are emerging as the new visionaries of Australia. They are building a blueprint of how to make delicious, age-worthy, food-friendly wines – one such outfit is De Bortoli.

Vittorio De Bortoli started producing in 1928, purely for his family and friends. Under the missionary zeal and relentless expansion of Deen De Bortoli, Vittorio's son, the brand was developed to where it is now – one of Australia's most successful and largest family wine companies. Sadly, Deen passed away suddenly in October 2003, and the company is now in the very capable hands of his children, Darren, Leanne, Kevin and Victor, and Leanne's husband Steve Webber. Whilst studying for her degree in wine marketing at the world-famous Roseworthy College in Adelaide, Leanne De Bortoli met Steve Webber at a party. Steve had already graduated with a wine degree. They are now joint managers of the Yarra Valley Estate, and Steve is chief winemaker at this world-renowned vineyard.

The family business has evolved to take advantage of the individual strengths of the many diverse regions across Australia. The original

winery is in Riverina, the agricultural heartland of Australia, home to one of De Bortoli's most highly acclaimed wines, Noble One. This is a Sauternes-style wine that's regarded as Australia's finest dessert wine, on a par with the great Sauternes and Barsac wines of Bordeaux. The De Bortolis recently acquired Hunter Valley winery produces iconic wine from the most widely known varieties, Semillon and Shiraz. However, it is their Yarra Valley vineyard that's causing the most global interest. It's here they produce consistently excellent Chardonnay and Pinot Noir. De Bortoli and some of its close Yarra neighbours, such as Yering Station and Coldstream Hills, are producing the country's finest examples of these sought-after grape varieties year-on-year, but the world's wine critics have begun to level criticism at the way that some Australian wines are made.

It's felt that some Australian winemakers are making faultless but sometimes characterless wines. Steve has identified this and has taken unprecedented steps to put the soul back into Aussie wines. So what is it that now sets them apart from their competitors? Steve explains:

'Our fundamental philosophy is that wine should have a sense of place. There has been a trend to identify and cherish the origin of good food, be it oysters, beef, cheese ... Now consumers are becoming more interested in the origin of their wine. My opinion is that wine should not taste of oak nor excessive extraction of tannin or alcohol, but should taste of the region.'

He says this philosophy begins first and foremost in the vineyard. 'We've moved towards a more organic, more physically demanding viticulture to achieve similar results to our premium French counterparts, not because the French way is the only way but because it achieves the desired results.'

De Bortoli have changed many of their finest vineyards to organic winemaking practices in the belief that better plant and soil health delivers better fruit quality in the grapes. The preservation of the vineyards is very important to the whole De Bortoli family, as it contributes to the priceless legacy they wish to pass on to their children.

Another change that Steve believes has made a huge difference to his wine style is to pick early. Winemakers in Australia are trained to pick their fruit as ripe as possible, often resulting in wines that are just too jammy. Steve has trained his pickers to harvest some of the grapes at the exact point when they are only just ripe. He believes that this adds edginess to the blend.

The De Bortoli Shiraz has led Steve down a different path to the traditional Australian oaked style of Shiraz: 'I believe most people do like oak in their wine, they just don't necessarily want to smell it or taste it.' They use barrels about twice the normal size, which contribute similar oak flavours in a far more subtle manner. He also adds subtle amounts of the white variety Viognier to his red blend, which adds perfume and complexity to the final wine.

The most significant difference in their wine is created in the winery itself, where, put simply, less is more. New World winemakers have a tendency to interfere and to control the process. However, Steve has found that the more gentle he and his team are with the fruit, the less they have to do, as nature begins to look after itself. This new, non-interventionist way of thinking, using gravity to move wine around where possible (some of his finished wines have never been through a pump) and using yeast found naturally in the vineyards rather than from a packet, has lead to a new motto in the winery: 'It is harder to do nothing.'

The De Bortoli Yarra Valley Estate is one of the favourite weekend destinations for the sophisticated Melbourne foodie set, and for the armies of wine tourists that come to the Yarra Valley every week. It's less than an hour from the fashionable eastern suburbs of Melbourne.

Leanne produces a quarterly newsletter, 'Le Quattro Stagioni', that keeps the many ardent followers of their cause up-to-date with affairs at the winery. There are many things to enjoy on the estate, an award-winning 'cellar door' tasting facility, and beautiful picnicking areas, but the apple in the eye of Leanne and Steve is the spectacular De Bortoli Yarra Valley restaurant. They recently recruited a chef from one of Sydney's top Italian restaurants to run things, and Leanne and Steve have been heaped with international gastronomical acclaim, including an award for the world's best winery restaurant.

SUSY ATKINS' EXPERT TIP

Matching Wine and Food by Region Another great way to find star food and wine matches is to stick to the same region for both. In other words, plan to serve, say, Italian food with an all-Italian cast of wines. It's amazing how well the rich pasta sauces and cheeses of Italy go with tangy, rich Italian red wines. But is it really so amazing that they complement each other, when you consider the food and wine have grown up together, evolving all the time so they work well in partnership? Other great regional matches are fresh shellfish and Loire Valley whites; Spanish red wine and lamb, a must-try in the Rioja region; paëlla and Spanish whites; grilled sardines and Portuguese Vinho Verde; creamy, pungent Burgundian cheeses and red Burgundy; goat's cheese and Sancerre, another Loire Valley match; Alsace whites and savoury tarts/quiches; Argentinian red wines and grilled steak; bone-dry fino sherry and tapas; Provencal rosés and garlicky grilled vegetables; Australian Shiraz with barbecued baby 'roo steaks – OK, I made that last one up!

The De Bortolis' love of all things Italian and their heritage is seen in their food, which concentrates on strictly seasonal day-fresh ingredients, in the style of Piedmont, north-west Italy. Rick Stein, Nick Nairn and Antonio Carluccio have cooked at some of the frequent gastronomical events at the restaurant, sealing its international reputation. No tour of Australia's wine regions would be complete without a trip to De Bortoli, and no tasting experience of Australian wine would be complete without the De Bortoli range.

Grape Variety
Syrah/Shiraz

Shiraz is the red wine equivalent of Chardonnay. It will grow just about anywhere and offers a large array of exciting flavours depending on where it is planted. It ripens early, which means that it can be harvested before any major disease or rain can spoil the fruit, which makes it popular with winemakers as well as drinkers! Flavour-wise, it has many different forms, the most famous Australian is the classic Barossa Shiraz. It's full of bramble and briar fruit, with a buttery, minty quality. If treated carefully, it is capable of producing world-class wines that can age beautifully for up to twenty years. It's hard to find a Shiraz wine with less than 14% alcohol!

You don't have to keep it to enjoy it. Some red wines, like Italy's Nebbiolo or France's Cabernet Sauvignon, need to be kept for a few years before they reveal their best qualities, but Syrah has a large 'window of drinking'. In other words, even the higher-end wines can be enjoyed less than a year after they have been bottled. However, the best wines really reward after a bit of patience, so try and keep them.

Syrah was brought to the Northern Rhône by a templar knight after the Crusades, where it thrived for over 700 years before being transported and planted all over the world.

Syrah or Shiraz is best known and loved for the great red wines of northern Rhône, namely Hermitage, Côte Rôtie and Cornas, and also the great Barossa reds of Australia, like Penfold's Grange. However, plantings are cropping up all over the world, in places like South Africa, Argentina and even Italy, all with signs of real potential.

AUSTRALIA DE BORTOLI IN THE YARRA VALLEY

Shiraz (Syrah in France) is the great grape of Châteauneuf-du-Pape and other Rhône wines. In the hands of the top Australian winemakers, like the De Bortoli family, it takes on extra warmth, richness and smoothness. The Australians broke new ground by putting the grape variety on the label and blending grapes from different regions to get the best wine.

Tasting Notes De Bortoli Shiraz

Susy Atkins

'Look beyond the obvious with this red: sure, there's the trademark Australian ripe fruit – bags of rich blackcurrant, in this case. You could be standing in a sun-baked vineyard as you smell the wine, but there's more here – a twist of black pepper, a hint of toffee, a sprinkling of spice – that makes it special.'

Joe Wadsack

'This is definitely the best example yet of this multi-flavoured but frighteningly gluggable wine. The fruit comes from three radically different areas, that each play a part in the end product. It smells of mulberries, cloves, and all-spice, while the flavour is pure blackberry crumble with custard.'

Jean-Marc Sauboua

'This is a simply delicious wine overflowing with flavour. Inky dark colour, ripe, rich and plush, with a lot of jammy plum, blackberry and spice. Finishes with a long, complex aftertaste and a gush of fruit. A real winner for a long winter evening. Drink now but you can keep for up to five years.'

Wine Style Guide Experiment with Taste

Nothing is more typical of Australian red than a cracking, full-blooded Shiraz like our featured De Bortoli wine. Australian Shiraz (known as Syrah in France) is the red grape variety on which the entire wine industry of this vast country is founded and it comes in many subtly different styles, so there are plenty of other examples to try. In its most basic form, Australian Shiraz produces a simple, no-nonsense red. But it's much better at the bargain end, to try blends of Shiraz with other grape varieties. If you like Shiraz, but you're on a budget, then go for a Shiraz–Cabernet or a Shiraz–Grenache. Here, the Shiraz doesn't have to be particularly special, because the other complementary flavours help make the wine a whole lot more interesting. Another variety to look out for is Mourvèdre, known as Mataro in Australia. This is a rich, firm variety that works brilliantly when paired with soft jammy Shiraz, to make an inexpensive but full and versatile red.

At the top of the quality ladder Aussie Shiraz is capable of a whole range of gorgeous wines. The ones from the coolest areas of Australia, like Pemberton in Western Australia and parts of Victoria, are famed for their amazing spiciness. Look out for pungent aromas of cracked black pepper and juniper, along with the sweet whiff of dried cherries. If you like this stuff, then try the wines from the spiritual home of this noble variety, the northern Rhône Valley in France. Wines made here from Syrah, like Crozes-Hermitage, Cornas and Côte-Rôtie, have a similar spiciness, but will be a touch more elegant, and although concentrated, usually less oaky.

If you discover you like ripe juicy Shiraz with a hint of spice, then some fantastic value can be had from the new examples made in Argentina and Chile. Food-wise, this more easy-going style seems perfectly suited to game, duck and dried meats. For fine complexity and almost European-style elegance, but plenty of ripe fruit, give New Zealand's Syrahs a whirl, especially the ones from the relatively warm Hawke's Bay region.

Of course, there's another type of Shiraz, the one that put Australia on the map, the big, bruising, blockbuster Shiraz. This is the monster wine that set the world alight about Aussie reds, and it traditionally comes from South Australia. For decades there have been two star wines, Henschke's Hill of Grace Shiraz, and Penfold's Grange. These are capable of ageing for many decades in bottle, and regularly fetch in excess of £1,000 per case of six bottles in auction whatever the vintage! The good news is that for around £10, you can buy other superb Shiraz from the Limestone Coast, Mudgee and Langhorne Creek regions, as they are still slightly under-valued. This is a perfect wine for Christmas turkey!

Try other big Shiraz from around the world too – notably, South Africa is making some impressive gutsy examples in its hotter vineyards. If you like hefty, chewy Shiraz styles, other wines that might appeal include oaky Malbecs from Argentina (see Chapter 12), with their black cherry fruit, good concentration and smoky-spicy hints. Try the big reds too from the Alentejo, Dão, Bairrada and Douro regions of Portugal, and Garnacha from Spain, perhaps from the Priorato region. Fans of reds with spicy undertones should get their hands on hearty Zinfandel from California (not the weedy pink stuff, but the

full-on red 'Zin'!) and do try Carmenere from Chile for another take on the savoury, earthy style of red.

Back in Europe, a thorough rummage around the rich reds of Southern France is a must – many are blends based on Syrah and in this hot climate, they offer a similar ripe, deeply fruity, full-bodied style to our Australian wine. And if you want to take things further into fine wine territory, don't miss the reds of Piedmont in northern Italy. Made from the Nebbiolo grape, they manage to be intense, with a full structure, yet beautifully perfumed and easy to match with food.

Starting Your Own Wine Collection

You're discovering how wonderful wine is and you want to begin your own collection. Great! But where to start? Our Wine Club selections have been chosen especially as a cost-effective starting point so you can taste along with us and compare notes with the experts as you work your way through the book. Apart from the Club selections, let's assume you are not a lottery winner and want to start a wine collection on a fairly tight budget. The good news is Britain is the best place in the world when it comes to shopping for wine. The UK is considered the 'shop window' of the wine world, as you can buy anything you like here. Here's the perfect purchase of three cases (thirty-six bottles) to kick off a general basic cellar. Case one: make sure you have everyday, easy-going whites and rosés (Sauvignon de Touraine, Vin de Pays d'Oc Chardonnay or Spanish Rosado), plus some special bottles of white for fine dining (New Zealand Sauvignon, good German Riesling and white Burgundy). Case two: reds – mix everyday drinking (perhaps inexpensive Côtes-du-Rhône reds or Aussie Cab – Shiraz blends) and splash out on a few bottles for special occasions (good Pinot Noir, red Bordeaux, Rioja). Complete your collection with a case of 'oddities' – bottles of cava for impromptu casual parties; one Champagne; pink fizz; port, dessert wine and dry sherry for great entertaining. Make sure to drink up the cheap and cheerful wines quickly; the others will keep for longer. Make tasting notes so you know what to buy again, and over time, build your collection on the styles you like most. Simple!

Chapter 8
South Africa
Featuring Jaques and Andre Bruwer in Robertson

Of all the diverse wine-producing regions of the world, the Western Cape – South Africa's wine country – is one of the most breathtakingly beautiful. Craggy mountains form a dramatic backdrop to verdant green vineyards, and state-of-the-art high-tech wineries sit close by traditional white Cape Dutch homesteads. The main wine regions – Stellenbosch, Paarl, Franschhoek and Constantia – are decidedly pretty; the coast is nearby, with whales often sighted at Hermanus, contrasting with the beckoning bright lights of Cape Town. If you want to go on a long-haul wine discovery trip, South Africa should be one of your first choices!

Gorgeous scenery aside, the South African wineries have struggled for a long time to get to the position they now hold. Back in the 1980s and early '90s, during the apartheid system of government, the wine industry closed in on itself – ironically, just as other key New World wine countries were bursting on to the international scene. So while Australian, Chilean and American wineries blossomed, and UK drinkers fell in love with their modern, fruity wines, South Africa fell behind drastically, producing far too many rough, nasty reds and bland or sweet whites.

UK drinkers were also boycotting South African wine in droves in protest at apartheid. As Aussie wines started to take over, the outlook for the Cape's wineries looked dismal. But since 1994, when Nelson Mandela became president of the 'Rainbow Nation', the winemakers of this newly vibrant, progressive country have caught up rapidly. Sales of South African wine in the UK have gone from almost zero to around 12 million cases per year, and the country is now the fifth most important wine producer here, selling more wine than Spain, Chile and Argentina!

South Africa's winelands are all centred around Cape Town in the south-west of the country. One key region is Stellenbosch, a large area often described as the powerhouse for production of big, hefty red wines. Stellenbosch town itself seems devoted to wine, with a wine college and all the wine shops, bars and fine

JEAN-MARC SAUBOUA'S EXPERT TIP

Wine has Legs!
Have you heard of a wine's "tears" or "legs"? As a winemaker I get a hint of the body and/or sweetness of a wine from its viscosity (liquids with a high viscosity are usually very thick and flow very slowly, while low-viscosity liquids are generally thin and flow quickly). To check this, just bring your glass to an upright position, give it a little shake or twirl and the wine will settle back, leaving trails down the side of the glass known as "tears" or "legs" (personally I prefer legs, maybe because I am French!). The less pronounced or obvious these are, with a Sauvignon Blanc or a light Beaujolais for instance, the less substantial the wine will be on the palate; the more pronounced, like a well-rounded Chardonnay or heavy Aussie Shiraz, the fuller the mouth will be. It's that easy – believe me!

restaurants you could hope for! Then there's Paarl, a slightly warmer spot which makes great Shiraz and Cabernet; Franschhoek, a pretty green valley within Paarl that seems to have an independent winemaking community of its own; Constantia, the oldest wine region dating from the 17th century, right by Cape Town, making great Sauvignon Blanc and Merlot; Robertson, further inland, with a limestone soil and a warm but breezy climate that's proving successful for top white wines; Walker Bay, a much cooler region on the coast where some of the best Pinot Noir is made; and Swartland, where sun-baked grapes make blockbuster reds.

In the past, the vineyards seemed to have all the wrong grape varieties – or if they were the right ones, they were in the wrong spots or had unhealthy, virus-infected plants. Now much more care is being taken to put the right varieties in the places where the soil and climate really suit them, and poorer varieties – or the many sick Cape vines – have gradually been replaced by more serious and healthy ones.

The winemakers are better equipped to make these decisions, partly because their wineries are now kitted out with modern, high-tech machinery and tanks, and partly because the new generation of producers have travelled abroad to other wine countries and worked in France, Australia or California, picking up the latest ideas and techniques along the way. Up to the early 1990s, South Africa played no part in the exchange of ideas that takes place between winemakers across the globe – now it most definitely does.

Whites have become cleaner and more characterful, with crisper, zestier, brighter flavours. Look out for impressive Chardonnays, bearing a lot of rich weight and oak, but with a fresh streak of acidity to balance out the richness. The fruity but crisp Sauvignon Blanc is wowing a lot of critics at the moment, and there are plenty of good-value, easy-drinking Chenin Blancs and Colombards for those who want to try some different varieties.

If anything, the reds have improved more dramatically. They are now packed with ripe, sometimes quite chunky, powerful fruit flavours and often they are carefully oak-aged to enhance the wine. The important red grapes grown here are mostly well-known international varieties. Cabernet Sauvignon is used to make lots of excellent reds, either on its own or in blends, as is Merlot. Shiraz is emerging only recently as a major star, producing intensely concentrated ripe flavours with plenty of spice and pepper in the mix.

If you were under the impression most South African reds were blockbusters, you'd be right, except for the more subtle, soft Pinot Noirs made in the cooler vineyard areas of the Cape. These can be very elegant. And don't miss Pinotage, South Africa's very own red grape, a cross between Pinot Noir and Cinsaut developed there in the 1920s. Pinotage used to be blamed, rightly, for much of the country's sour, rough red, but now it turns out a high number of juicy, plummy reds that range from big and hearty to more simple and easy-drinking.

There is even a new group of red wines, called Cape Blends, that are a mix of mainly Pinotage blended with Cabernet Sauvignon, Cabernet Franc, Merlot or Shiraz.

If you want to taste through South Africa's wide range of wine styles, you also need to try their fun, frivolous sparklers, sweet and fortified wines, although you may have to go there to find a great selection as they aren't all exported. Whatever you're trying from the Cape, South Africa does appear to be good value for money. Although there are still a few boring or rough wines in the cheapest price brackets, once you hit £5 some exciting, ripe flavours start to shine through, and at around £8 you can get a serious bottle that looks like a bargain besides similar wines from the rest of the world. Yes, the days when South Africa was the outsider in the wine world are definitely over.

It's also good to see Fair Trade projects finally taking off in parts of the Cape. In the past, only white workers and managers rose to the senior positions in South African vineyards and wineries. Almost all black workers rented their shacks and had no stake in the wine company they worked for. Today, in some progressive wineries, this is all changing, with 'black empowerment' projects giving the more menial workers a share in the profits and the chance to train,

SUSY ATKINS' EXPERT TIP

Crowd Pleasers
It's all very well talking about the perfect wine for a particular dish, but what about when you're faced with a wide range of dishes, either a buffet, or when a crowd is out to eat in a restaurant and everyone orders different things? Some wines are more versatile than others and they go effortlessly with lots of dishes and clash with very little. These wines tend to be medium-bodied, well-balanced, straightforward styles – not the biggest, most individual characters around, perhaps, but the sort of easy-drinking, fruity wines that should please everyone. Here are the best all-rounders. Whites: South African Chenin Blanc; Pinot Blanc from Alsace in France; simple dry whites from south-west France; German and New World Riesling; unoaked or lightly oaked Chardonnays; light, dry, Italian whites like Verdicchio, Orvieto and Soave. Reds: Pinot Noir (from anywhere); soft inexpensive Merlot; Australian Cabernet-Shiraz blends; Argentinian Malbec; Italian Chianti; Spanish Rioja; Southern Italian reds; cheaper Rhône reds. Don't forget versatile dry rosés with lighter savoury summer food, and the best all-purpose, good-value fizz – Spanish cava! Pick these wines and you'll get a higher proportion of guests complimenting your choice.

SOUTH AFRICA JAQUES AND ANDRE BRUWER IN ROBERTSON

move up the pay scale and secure an independent future. For one such example, look no further than Fairview, a winery which has its own Fair Trade initiatives, as its founder Charles Back is one of the most enlightened and forward-thinking (not to mention philanthropic) winemakers in the Cape.

Good news came a couple of years ago when an agreement was signed with the EU allowing South Africa to export a proportion of wine free of customs duty, a move which has led to more funding for ethical trading initiatives.

Things should improve further in South African wine, not only conditions for workers but also (and perhaps because of this) better quality at the baseline, so that the cheapest wines are a bit more characterful, and even more flavour is packed into the Chenins, Colombards and Pinotages. We predict South Africa will continue to make rapid progress, as it has done over the past decade or so. Then maybe the prices will rise, so snap up those bargain, mid-priced wines while you can!

Grower Profile
Jacques and Andre Bruwer

Many of the Cape's wine regions lie near the coast where the hot sun is tempered by cooling breezes. Robertson, the base of Jacques and Andre Bruwer is much further inland, 150 km from Cape Town and alongside the Breede river. It's warmer here, and some might be surprised that good wine can be made in such a hot spot. But taste Robertson's top wines – especially its stunning whites – and you'll see why it's now hailed as one of the most exciting regions in South Africa.

In fact, Robertson is known as the 'valley of wine and roses'. Vibrant flowers grow alongside healthy vineyards, partly to do with the excellent soils here – stony with a high limestone content – and partly because of the unique climate of the region. It's warm and sunny, yes, but fanned in places by a cool, south-easterly breeze during the summer afternoons and evenings, with misty, even chilly nights, which help safeguard the more delicate aromas and flavours of the grapes.

The Bruwer family moved here to take over a farm in 1927. They picked a wonderful spot, where the lazy, meandering Klaas Voogds river joins the larger Breede river, 9 km from Robertson town, on

the road to Bonnievale. This classic and serene Dutch Cape homestead dates back to 1818. The Bruwers are originally from the Loire Valley, one of France's most important wine-producing regions, so it's hardly surprising they spotted the potential of the terroir for vineyards.

Willie, the patriarch of the family, planted vines including Chenin Blanc (known here as Steen) and Muscadel, and at first sold his wine to a huge South African co-operative for bottling. Willie's son Andre joined his father in the vineyards in 1965 and took over the reins in 1974. He's still at the helm and has transformed Bon Courage into the premium wine producer it is today.

Andre is totally dedicated to the farm and sees himself very much as a farmer of grapes. He's often found on his motorbike, straw hat firmly on against the relentless sun, driving up and down the vineyards, looking for things to improve or correct. He hates to be away for more than a few days. Andre modernised the winery and cellar in the 1970s, bringing in new equipment. Then he extended the estate by purchasing the neighbouring farm in 1983. It was Andre who renamed the estate 'Bon Courage', a translation of its original name, Goedemoed.

In 1990, Jacques, Andre's son, joined the family firm. Like his father, he's a graduate of the famous Elsenburg Agricultural College near Stellenbosch, where many of South Africa's top winemakers are trained. Jacques also spent time working in France and Germany, an experience typical of the new generation of well-travelled Cape winemakers. Jacques brought new ideas to the winemaking side of the operation, and gradually focused more on the vinification in the cellar, while his father concentrated on the vineyards – it's a truly complementary family team.

Jacques is considered one of the most innovative winemakers in the Robertson area and is a champion of 'cold-temperature' white-winemaking – using cooling methods to keep the grape juice and wine as fresh as possible while it is being made. Although still young,

JOE WADSACK'S EXPERT TIP

Chilling Wine in the Great Outdoors
On a picnic? Haven't got a fridge handy? How do you chill your wine? Here are a couple of tips to help. Number one – when going to the beach, always take a tea towel. If you have a bottle to chill (and in the height of summer, this could apply just as well to red wine) then dip the towel in the sea and wrap the bottle with it. Stick the bottle neck down into the sand in full sun – if you can locate a breezy spot, even better. Although it takes quite a lot of time, something you probably have plenty of at the beach, when the towel is dry the wine wrapped inside will be sufficiently cold to drink. Second tip – if you are by a stream, find a particularly fast-moving part, if you can. Tie a bottle to the bank – onto a branch or something – and place the wine into the stream. Even if the water is relatively warm, the movement of the water past the bottle will chill the wine very effectively in minutes.

he has certainly had his share of recognition, with an array of medals and awards for Bon Courage wines. He is particularly fond of the sparkling wine he makes at the estate.

Andre is no stranger to awards either, collecting many of the top trophies in his time, including overall winner (for best gold and double gold medals) in the 2003 Veritas Show, South Africa's largest annual wine competition. Both men like to go deep-sea fishing to relax in what little spare time they have.

So what makes Bon Courage so special? The vineyards seem to produce particularly healthy grapes, and need no pesticide sprays, due to the healthy Robertson climate. Moreover, the grapes are always picked at night, as Andre believes strongly in harvesting at cool temperatures to retain freshness and the delicate aromas they strive for. He is also a master at irrigation, which is vital in an area which sees so little rain. Andre controls the water supply to the grapes very carefully so that the plants are slightly stressed and thirsty. This leads to more concentrated flavours and aromas in the fruit at harvest time – less water = more fruit flavour! So does keeping the grape yields low – the Bruwers keep only the best bunches on each vine, weeding out the weaker grapes throughout the season.

One factor in their huge success is the consistency and strength of the father and son team. 'We don't believe in hiring different winemakers, who will only leave for a better salary after a year or two,' say the Bruwers. Andre's extraordinary relationship with his vineyards and his close involvement in Jacques' work ensure that his son always gets the very best grapes possible to work with. Add in Jacques' highly modern, cutting-edge techniques in the winery and you have the dream team!

Grape Variety
Colombard

Many of us have probably sipped a drink based on Colombard before now and not realised – it's one of the three grape varieties traditionally used for Cognac production. So if you enjoy the occasional digestif of fine French brandy, you've already enjoyed something created in part by Colombard!

It's also a mainstay of popular, inexpensive whites from the south-west of France, although you will rarely see the name Colombard anywhere on the label. Crack open a crisp, fresh, young Vin de Pays des Côtes de Gascogne white, however, and there's almost certainly Colombard in the blend. VDP Côtes de Gascogne is very popular in the UK and usually good value for money. This vine is grown across France's south-west and used in other simple, light white blends.

Colombard has been widely used to make brandy and table wine in California and South Africa too. It is often called French Colombard in California, and was the state's most widely planted grape of all in the 1970s, although Chardonnay has since overtaken it spectacularly. But for a long time Colombard held sway, making huge amounts of typically refreshing and lightly fruity, if fairly simple, white wine for everyday drinking. In South Africa, some winemakers have started to take it more seriously, using modern methods in the winery to keep the essential freshness of the grape, while coaxing more aroma and zesty citrus flavours out of it. The Robertson region currently leads the way.

WINE OF SOUTH AFRICA

2005

BON COURAGE

ESTATE

COLOMBARD
ROBERTSON - WINE OF ORIGIN

GROWN & PRODUCED ON BON COURAGE WINE ESTATE
BY ANDRE BRUWER AND HIS SON JACQUES

ESTATE WINE

SELECTED & SHIPPED BY THE IMPORTER DWL RG7 4PL UK CONTAINS SULPHIL

750ml B 60mm

Often found in white wine blends, the South Africans have let Colombard stand tall and made it their own. Why? Well, it has ocean-fresh aromas of lemon grass, citrus and apples with mouth-watering Sauvignon-like zippy flavours. Great with seafood, for summer drinking or as an aperitif.

Tasting Notes Bon Courage Colombard

Susy Atkins
'The important thing here is the crisp, mouth-watering, zesty lemon–tangerine flavour, which tastes a bit like biting into fresh citrus fruit. It shows what delicious flavours can be coaxed out of a grape that can, in the wrong hands, taste a bit bland. This wine has a really fruity, dry and refreshing style and would be a perfect aperitif.'

Joe Wadsack
'Colombard is totally underrated in this country. It doesn't have the kudos of Sauvignon Blanc, but this example has the same lip-smacking, first-Granny-Smith-off-the-tree taste. Get the oysters out! Reminds me of a summer evening in Quay at Bordeaux, thinking how lucky I am that I do this for a living. Cracking!'

Jean-Marc Sauboua
'Gorgeous purity and clarity, not a flashy wine but its delicate frame hides dense flavours of tangerine, pie crust, lime and some mineral character. Very appealing wine. Not a blockbuster but sleek and focused, it's a delicious aperitif! Drink chilled now and for one year after vintage.'

Wine Style Guide Experiment with Taste

Our featured South African Colombard is crisp, aromatic and unoaked with a dry finish. Start by trying other dry whites from the Western Cape to compare. Sauvignon Blanc would be a good place to begin. South African Sauvignon has won much praise in recent vintages for its good balance and refreshing flavours. It tends to be more fruity than Sauvignon from France's Loire Valley, but less pungent and ripe than New Zealand's famous style of white. Look out for flavours of lemon, gooseberry, even passion fruit, in Cape Sauvignons. Try one from the Constantia region, on the outskirts of Cape Town, or one from Robertson – the regions will be on the label.

Then there's Chenin Blanc, a must-try if you are exploring South African white wines. Cape Chenin is often an easy-drinking, unoaked white with a juicy apple and guava flavour, sometimes with a very slight hint of sweetness. It makes a good comparison with Colombard. Watch out for some richer, oakier styles too.

South African Chardonnay will, on the whole, taste altogether bigger, riper and creamier than Colombard, Sauvignon and Chenin, so it isn't as similar, although you might find a Colombard–Chardonnay blend that's worth investigating.

For the French take on Colombard, try dry white wines from the south-west of France, especially Vin de Pays des Côtes de Gascogne (usually blended with Ugni Blanc and possibly other grapes). These wines can taste crisp and grassy but they don't last – drink them up quickly! Once you've tried South African Chenin Blanc, check out Loire whites made from the same grape variety. Vouvray is a good example, but bear in mind it is sometimes dry, often medium-dry and occasionally can be medium-sweet. Typical tasting notes for Vouvray have apples and walnuts in the flavour.

Delve further into the world of aromatic, unoaked whites with a close look at the fascinating range from Alsace in north eastern France. Try Alsace Pinot Blanc in particular, which is a crowd-pleasing, appley wine that goes extremely well with a wide range of food. It should appeal to you, as should the dry light whites of Italy – turn back to Chapter 5 for a closer look at Orvieto and some other suggestions for exploring similar Italian styles.

Other wines that should be on your shopping list are: German Rieslings, with their lovely crisp, fresh, light fruit flavours; Argentinian Torrontes (more about that in chapter twelve) for its lovely perfume and grapey, lemony, slightly spicy notes; and even English white wines, which have improved hugely of late and now tend to have whistle-clean, freshly chopped orchard fruits and a floral, hedgerow blossom aromas. Then there's the little-known but utterly moreish Grüner Veltliner, which makes Austria's slightly peppery, lemony-fresh dry whites. Give these interesting white wines a chance – it's worth it to escape from endless bottles of Chardonnay!

Wine and Calories

It's normal to cut down on wine when you're on a diet – but why? Can wine really contribute to being fat? Unfortunately, yes! A glass of wine contains anything from around 70 to 150 calories, or even more if you use a big glass! The alcohol and sugar account for the calories, and if you drink several glasses of wine a night, not only should you look out for your liver, but your waistline might well suffer too. Happily, we can be clever and enjoy a glass of wine that has fewer calories than usual. Here's how: Obviously, drink a smaller glass – some bars now serve 250ml measures of wine, which is one-third of a normal bottle. Stick to the old 125ml measurement (and don't double the rounds!). Then pick the right style of wine. Some are naturally lower in alcohol, and therefore calories. A good example is German Riesling, which often weighs in at around 9% or 10% alcohol, instead of many New World whites which might be as much as 14.5%. But be careful to pick a dry style of wine – a sweet German Riesling will carry more calories! So, choose dry wines and look at the label for the alcohol content. Champagne isn't especially strong at around 12%, and it usually comes in fairly small 'flute' glasses, while 'brut' on a Champers label tells you it is dry – so if you're counting calories how about a glass of fizz? It's a great excuse!

Chapter 9
New Zealand
Featuring Babich in Auckland

Several New World wine countries have become known to us through a range of modern wines using a group of very well-known grapes – Chardonnay, of course, and Merlot or Cabernet. New Zealand, though, is different. The Kiwis arrived on the international wine scene with one unforgettable style of wine – Marlborough Sauvignon Blanc.

Once you've tried Sauvignon Blanc made in the region of Marlborough, on New Zealand's South Island, your view of white wine may be altered forever. It might not be something you want to drink every day because of the sheer force of strong flavours and aromas, but you certainly won't forget this extraordinary and extrovert wine. For a start, it's wonderfully aromatic – swirl your glass and you barely have to sniff at all to catch a rich aroma of ripe gooseberry, tomato leaf, freshly mown grass, juicy tropical fruits, asparagus, herbs . . .

The palate is zingy and fresh with mouth-watering acidity and loads of that tangy gooseberry flavour lingering on. This is certainly a wine that's easy to spot in a 'blind' tasting. And it's miles away from the more subtle, lean, lemony Sauvignons of France.

So how did such a new and distinctive style of Sauvignon emerge? It's got a lot to do with New Zealand's cool climate, combined with the fact there's plenty of sunshine too. If it's a good year, the Sauvignon Blanc grapes ripen nicely by day, developing lots of flavour, but at night the temperature drops dramatically, so that fresh acidity and a mouth-watering aroma are retained in the fruit. All this means the finished wine has bags of concentrated fruitiness but a fresh, distinctive crisp streak running through it too. Marlborough has a particularly cool, sunny climate, and it also has the sort of hard, stony soils which suit the development of intensely flavoured grapes for white wine.

The best New Zealand wines have a very fruity, clean and pure personality: it's almost as if all that fresh air and wide-open green space is reflected in the crisp, fruit-salad flavours of the wine! So when you're sampling New Zealand wines, by all means start with the famous Sauvignon Blanc, but they use other grapes, so don't miss the often well-balanced citrusy Chardonnay, the mouth-watering Riesling, spicy Gewurztraminer and peachy Pinot Gris. They can be just as good! In general, expect richer styles in the warmer North Island vineyard areas, and lighter, crisper whites from the South Island cool spots.

That cool climate has made it harder for the Kiwis to develop impressive reds. It's tricky to get full ripeness into the reds in many parts of the country and for a long time New Zealand's reds lagged

behind its whites, with lots of bottles, especially the Cabernet Sauvignons, tasting disappointingly lean, under-ripe and stalky. Put it this way, do you actually want runner-bean flavour in your red wine? Thought not.

The New Zealanders took the hint and started to put more effort into red wines. Some Cabernet Sauvignon grapes were replaced with more Merlot and Pinot Noir, which suited the climate better and produced juicier, more appealing reds. Hotter locations were chosen for premium reds – Hawke's Bay on the North Island and Waiheke Island, a little dot of land out from Auckland, have proved good for richer reds, especially Merlot and Syrah. Other areas, like Martinborough and Marlborough, not to mention the newly planted Central Otago, have shown they can make serious reds from Pinot Noir, a difficult grape which needs just the right conditions. Indeed, New Zealand Pinot Noir is now very highly thought of, and can probably only be bettered by top examples from Burgundy and California. 'Bordeaux' blends (Cabernet with Merlot) have proved successful too, especially in warmer years.

The New Zealanders are now experts at getting their grapes as ripe as they can in their climate. They've mastered a technique known as 'canopy management', where they cut back the canopy of leaves to expose the grapes to the warm sun. This is used for both white and red grapes when necessary, and has proved a success in getting more juicy ripe flavour into the wines there.

Don't miss New Zealand's great-value sparkling wines. That cool climate comes in handy again – grape growing in lower temperatures produces the right sort of high-acid base wine from which good, fresh sparkling is made (see page 314 for more on this). Cool Marlborough, in particular, certainly turns out a crop of impressive bubblies, with that pure fruity character so typical of New Zealand wines.

Think of Wine as a Condiment
Now that you are more familiar with grape varieties, it helps to think of wine as a condiment when food matching. Although a lot of wine goes OK with a lot of food, some matches are heavenly and somehow seem to enhance both food and wine. One simple but canny way to achieve this is to pick wines from grape varieties which have the same qualities as a sauce or flavouring that naturally goes well with the food. It follows that if a dish is great with a squeeze of lemon on it, then a lemony white will work too – for example, with plain fresh white fish. Another good example is lamb, which is delicious with redcurrant sauce and mint sauce, and happens to be a great match with Cabernet Sauvignon, which has a red-berry and sometimes even minty character. Beef is often enjoyed with a peppery sauce, so why not try pairing it with Shiraz/Syrah, a red grape that has a distinctive peppery note? And it should go without saying that all sweet courses that would benefit from a drizzle of honey are divine with a honeyed, luscious dessert wine.

Interestingly, the cool climate means that picking a good vintage might be important when choosing these wines. Some of the regions here struggle in poor years. At best, during a warm year, they produce extremely elegant, complex flavours, miles away from the jammy, overblown, alcoholic styles of some hot spots in the world. But in poor years, frost can be a serious problem, leading to a terrible loss in grapes. Back in 2003, the crop was badly affected by frost, and in some places over 60% of the grape harvest was lost! That doesn't necessarily mean it's a bad year for quality (in fact, the wines that were made in 2003 were generally high quality), but it might mean some of your favourite wines from that vintage are in short supply. So watch out, especially if you are buying expensive fine wines, as some years might see fluctuations in quality, just as in some other cooler parts of the world. Talk to an expert wine merchant, or invest in a pocket guide to international wine vintages to get exactly the wine you want.

The shortages caused by frost have caused the Kiwis some headaches over the past few years, but nevertheless there has been something of a 'gold rush' to plant vines in New Zealand recently. This is still a young wine industry, and it is expanding at a great rate. In 1990, there were 131 wineries there; now there are over 500! The renowned Marlborough region is now wall-to-wall vines, and a fashionable new wine region like Central Otago is seeing huge investment. It will be interesting to see if a flood of new, possibly cheaper, New Zealand wines appear in the next few years from all the young vineyards, or if Mother Nature continues to keep the yields low.

For now, New Zealand wine prices are relatively high – the average bottle sold in the UK costs just under £6 which is higher than for any other country (the average price of a bottle of wine is just £3.79). This doesn't mean this wine isn't good value – it's just that the Kiwis don't do 'bargain basement' plonk, they trade in more serious wine. The bottles may have

JOE WADSACK'S EXPERT TIP

Alcohol Content
Alcohol content can vary enormously in wine. Some light, sweet German wines can have as little as 7% by volume, and some blockbuster Californian and Australian wines can have as much as 16% or more! The amount of alcohol in the wine directly relates to how ripe the grapes were when they were picked. It is a common misnomer that the higher the alcohol the better the wine. Now that we are drinking so much wine from the New World, it has become clear that we can have too much of a good thing. Wines that have loads of alcohol can taste over the top, too sweet and, contrary to the old wives' tales, may not age very well either. In reality, most of the dry reds and whites that I drink are between 12.5 and 14% alcohol. Dry red any lower than this is likely to be weedy and unripe, and wines that are above 14% can be a little tiring and oily, so are hardly ideal for serving at weddings! Remember, though, that this is just a guide and there are always exceptions to the rule.

quite high price tags but they are, on the whole, remarkably reliable, consistent and tasty, which makes them a good value buy.

One winery is particularly famous: Cloudy Bay, in Marlborough, has become a 'cult' label, competing for attention on top restaurant wine lists with more established celebrated wines from France, Italy and Spain. It was one of the first to produce the signature Marlborough Sauvignon Blanc and it did it brilliantly, creating a ripe, rich, complex version. Cloudy Bay Sauvignon is still one of the best examples, but its price can reflect its fame and the small amount available in this country. There are now plenty of other great Sauvignons that cost less – our featured Babich Sauvignon from Marlborough is highly regarded too, and it comes from one of New Zealand's most respected winemaking families. Other superb New Zealand wineries include Villa Maria, Craggy Range, Wither Hills, Hunters, Jackson Estate, Seresin, Sileni, Cable Bay, Felton Road and Goldwater. Even the giant of the country's industry, Montana, is reckoned by experts to be more than competent. So by all means try the cult label, but do be aware that standards run high in this wine land and there are great wines to be had from other, less well-known labels.

That's why it's important to sample wines from several different areas – start with Marlborough for those famous Sauvignons and other white wines, plus Pinot and sparkling. Then work your way round the South Island labels, including those from the Waipara area near Christchurch (great aromatic whites) and deeply fashionable, far-flung Central Otago (brilliant Chardonnays and Pinots but at high prices); then head to the North Island for the Martinborough area (classy Pinot Noir), Hawke's Bay (the best rich reds), Gisborne (good Chardonnay) and Waiheke Island (famous for Bordeaux blends). We guarantee it will be an enjoyable part of your wine education.

Grower Profile Babich

In 1910, a fourteen-year-old boy called Josip Babich left Croatia on the long and difficult journey to New Zealand, where he planned to start a new life with his brothers. Josip was escaping terrible hardship and conflict in Croatia, and he knew he would never see his parents again. He eventually arrived in the North Island of New Zealand to take up work digging and selling gum from kauri trees.

Inspired by his memories of the vineyards back home, in 1912 Josip planted his first vines on the terraces above the Kaikino swamp gum field. Four years later, he and his brothers made their first wine, selling it in cask and bottle under the name Babich Brothers. Back then, New Zealand's wine trade was pretty basic and almost all its wine was consumed in the country. Josip would tread the grapes with his feet, and travel for miles by horseback to sell a few bottles slung over the saddle. By the 1920s, he was selling fortified wines not only in bottles, but in half-gallon jars and big clay casks on the streets of Auckland. By then, the family also owned orchards and sold a variety of fruit as well as grapes.

Fast-forward to the 1940s, and the Babichs were increasingly focused on winemaking. By now, Josip's sons, Peter and Joe Junior, had become involved in the family business, and Babich Wines was transformed from a small, fortified wine producer into a modern winery that's renowned for world-class table wines. Josip died in 1983, and is remembered as one of the pioneers of the modern New Zealand wine trade. Interestingly, three of the country's largest wine companies, Montana, Villa Maria and Nobilo, all originated as small Croatian family businesses, so New Zealand has a lot to thank these enterprising immigrants for!

Today, Babich is one of the largest family-owned wineries, and a new generation has come on board, with Peter's son David joining the firm in 2001. Peter and Joe have only ever worked for Babich Wines, Peter for an astounding fifty-eight years (these days he's chairman of the company) and Joe for forty-eight as winemaker. Both have lived on Babich Road for their entire lives, first at Josip's house, then at their own places further up the street. They work brilliantly together, according to David, forming a great partnership that has lasted half a century.

'Both are strongly traditional in their approach to winemaking,' David continues. 'We will generally take a few years to determine how a vineyard performs, then start to make the style of wine that best suits that fruit. Often wineries will attempt to force a style on a vineyard, and it just doesn't work.' Babich Wines wants to produce fruit-driven, subtle wines that are not excessively manipulated by the winemaker. Joe recalls learning sound winemaking principles and integrity from his father Josip. 'For instance, stretching the supply of wine with water was once a common practice in New Zealand, but Dad was never one to try and make wine with anything other than grapes!' he says.

'You can't put flavour into grapes – it has to be there to start with,' continues Joe. 'The winemaker can only enhance it or spoil it.'

JEAN-MARC SAUBOUA'S EXPERT TIP

Location, Location, Location

Ever thought about planting a vineyard to make your own wine? Well, you'll only be successful if the region you live in lies between latitudes 30 and 50 degrees north and south of the equator. I am sorry o say that means Manchester and Birmingham will not be rivalling St-Emilion, Rioja or Tuscany unless we have a major climate shift! Between 30 and 50 degrees, the grapes will ripen satisfactorily to make a good wine. There is a wide range of climates in this zone; for example, in the consistently cool, damp conditions of southern England and Germany, it is sometimes difficult for the grapes to ripen fully. At the other extreme, in the hot, dry North African countries such as Morocco and Algeria, the problems are too much heat and insufficient rain, leading to over-ripe grapes with low acidity. The local geography will also affect the climate surrounding individual vineyards – northern hemisphere vineyards planted on south-facing slopes will be warmer because of increased exposure to the sun, and the proximity to large bodies of water can increase humidity and moderate changes in temperature. If an ideal climate were ever to exist, it would include sufficient moisture and warmth to enable the vines to grow and the grapes to ripen. I am still running all over the world to find it!

That philosophy has seen the Babich family range far beyond its roots in Henderson, on the North Island, in a quest for good vineyard land. Babich Wines now owns vineyards in the best regions of New Zealand's two islands, and has land both in warm areas, like Hawke's Bay, where the grapes for its rich 'flagship' red 'The Patriarch' are grown, and cool climate spots, like Marlborough, where the Sauvignon Blanc, Riesling, Pinot Gris and Pinot Noir come from.

Sauvignon Blanc is certainly the undisputed king of grape varieties for the family. In fact, Sauvignon Blanc from the Marlborough region makes up nearly two-thirds of their entire production, even though the family produces over fifteen different wines. 'I believe Marlborough makes the best Sauvignon Blanc in the world,' says David. 'When I show the wine to people around the world, they cannot believe the intensity of fruit flavour carried in it. But there's more to New Zealand than this one style. In the future there will be huge demand for other aromatic whites, as well as Pinot Noir and Syrah.'

Much of their success is down to the fact these are straightforward, pragmatic people. Peter says, when his father, Josip, first moved over from Croatia, 'he looked at someone on a bike and thought, "Will I ever own one of those?"'

'At our heart we have strong agricultural roots, dating back hundreds of years,' says David. This attitude is expressed in the way Peter and Joe like to do business. They tend not to have contracts – agreements are based on a handshake because both parties feel there is a benefit in working together. Perhaps this is becoming an outdated notion these days, but it has certainly served them well!

Grape Variety
Sauvignon Blanc

Sauvignon Blanc's popularity seems to be on the rise, and little wonder, as it often seems to make such wonderfully refreshing, zesty, aromatic white wines. They are usually unoaked too, so for anyone a bit fed up of oaky Chardonnays, this would be a good place to go.

The Loire Valley in France's cool central-north and Bordeaux, further south-west, were traditionally considered the first homes for Sauvignon Blanc. Some of France's most celebrated white wines – for example, Sancerre and Pouilly-Fumé (pronounced 'poo-ey foo-may') are made from 100% Sauvignon Blanc, and around Bordeaux some great blends with Semillon are produced. Some of these are rich and oaky; others major on the light, crisp and grassy style. But French Sauvignon Blanc has had to look to its laurels with the rise of a modern classic, New Zealand Sauvignon Blanc, which has effectively created a whole new take on this grape.

It was only thirty years ago that the first Sauvignon Blanc grapes were planted in Marlborough, on New Zealand's South Island, but the amazing concentration of rich aroma and flavour produced here has taken the wine world by storm. Some people find the extrovert blast of zesty, pungent fruit in Marlborough Sauvignon a bit tiresome after a while, but there are plenty of fervent fans of this distinctive type of wine.

Other regions of New Zealand have excelled with Sauvignon too, and there are fine (if a bit more subtle) versions made in other parts of the New World, but notably South Africa, which has recently proved it can make a well-balanced style of wine from this grape which looks set to be a bigger hit in the future.

Tasting Notes Babich Sauvignon Blanc

Susy Atkins

'Take a moment or two to savour the enticing, exotic aroma of this wine – I found gooseberries, pears, melons, tangerines and a herbaceous, chopped grass note all in there! The flavour is fresh and very fruity – like a cocktail of tropical fruits with an underlying tang of green gooseberry, and there's a mouth-watering full finish which lingers on the palate.'

Joe Wadsack

'New Zealand put this grape variety back on the map about fifteen years ago, and you can see why. This wine literally reeks of guava and passion fruit, and the taste is of freshly cut mango and peach. Yup, it's a flipping fruit salad for grown ups! Drink with Thai green curry or a tomatoey pasta dish.'

Jean-Marc Sauboua

'Lovely fruit jumps out of this glass. Aromas and flavours of gooseberry, fresh grass and melon permeate this fresh, brisk white. Sauvignon Blanc in all its splendour, I can drink bottles of it! Firmly structured and focused, it will make a tasty aperitif or the best partner to oysters, shellfish and smoked salmon. Drink cold now ... and without waiting, don't keep for more than a year or two from vintage.'

Sauvignon Blanc is the signature grape of New Zealand. The burning sun, bright blue skies and cool nights give a real intensity of flavour different to its European ancestors. It leads to ripe passion fruit, gooseberries and fresh-cut grass jumping out of the glass! The wines are fresh, vibrant but rich and round, with great flavour concentration and terrific balance. This is a good example to get the measure of this grape's performance in New Zealand.

Babich

2005

Family Reserve

SAUVIGNON BLANC

MARLBOROUGH

bottled by Babich Wines Ltd, Babich Road, Henderson, New Zealand
Imported by DWL
RG7 4PL, UK

%vol

e750ml

WINE OF NEW ZEALAND
CONTAINS SULPHITES

Wine Style Guide Experiment with Taste

New Zealand Sauvignon Blanc certainly isn't short on personality – in fact, there aren't really any other white wines that can match it for sheer force of perfume and punchy flavour. So if you like this style of wine, you clearly like whites with lots of upfront bright fruity character! However, there are other whites with forceful aromas, and similar unoaked but tangy, juicy characteristics. Here's how to find them:

Start off by tasting Sauvignon Blanc from other parts of New Zealand – Central Otago, Gisborne, Hawke's Bay and Martinborough, then head over to Australia and compare the famous Kiwi style with not-so-famous, rarer Aussie examples. Next, make sure you try other new-wave Sauvignons from Chile – try to get one from the Casablanca Valley region; California – but watch out for those labelled Fumé Blanc as this is a different, oakier style; and South Africa – Constantia is a good region to look for. Are the new Zealand wines really the most extrovert and 'in-yer-face', or are some of these other countries producing similar styles?

Of course, France's Sauvignon Blanc must be compared with the New Zealand style. To do this properly, you'll need to try Sauvignons from the Loire Valley – Sancerre and Pouilly-Fumé should be lean and elegant, though may be pricey; try Sauvignon de Touraine for a less expensive version – and from around Bordeaux and the south-west, where many might be blended with Semillon, but are still made in a grassy, lemony style.

Other interesting Sauvignons hail from northern Italy – the Alto Adige, Trentino areas; Austria, and the south of France. As you taste your way around these variations on the Sauvignon theme, ask yourself which are the richest, ripest, and which are the most subtle and light. Do you prefer one or the other, or a style that sits somewhere in between?

There's a wonderful world of other aromatic, slightly spicy white wines out there, so move on to sample more varieties that roughly fit the same category of wine. First off, Gewurztraminer is essential tasting for anyone who likes New Zealand Sauvignon Blanc, as it's also highly perfumed and exotic, with an amazing aroma of lychees and peaches, ginger and rosewater. Gewurz can be wonderful stuff, with a rich, ripe texture and fresh fruit flavour, but it is not for everyone, and you need to shell out more than a fiver for a good one – cheap Gewurz can be nastily reminiscent of floral air freshener! Try examples from Alsace, north-eastern France, Germany, Chile or even New Zealand again, which is doing well with this heady variety.

Other aromatic whites include Irsai Oliver, which makes good-value rose-scented whites in Eastern Europe; dry Muscat, a grapey-fresh summer quaffer; Tokay-Pinot Gris from Alsace, which can be wonderfully ripe, opulent and peachy; and limey-apricotty Albarino from western Spain, which is a 'cult' variety for some and probably Spain's best white grape. Riesling is a must-try too – especially the ripe, juicy, tangy Australian and New Zealand Rieslings, which have enough bright fruit flavours to satisfy a Sauvignon Blanc drinker. You should even try the underrated but incredibly refreshing dry sherries of Spain. Sounds surprising? Fino and manzanilla sherries are pale, lemony and bone-dry with a wonderful, almost salty, tang. Served fresh and cold, they always appeal to fans of zippy Sauvignon-style white wines.

Aromatic dry whites are refreshing and crisp enough to be enjoyed on their own, or pair them with simple fish and shellfish dishes, but save those with the strongest, brightest personalities (and that certainly includes New Zealand Sauvignon Blanc) to match with equally vivacious, brightly flavoured dishes like seared tuna and salsa; garlic prawns with lemon squeezed on them; grilled white fish with roast red peppers; pan-fried scallops and asparagus. Gewurztraminer goes well with sweet and sour Chinese food as well as mild Thai dishes and try the lighter, leaner, minerally Sauvignons and Rieslings with mild cheeses, particularly pairing Sancerre and goat's cheese for a classic match!

What's on the Label?

Although some wine labels have more marketing blurb on them than anything else (who really wants to know about 'the babbling brook running through the vineyards'?), there are certain useful facts to be found on a bottle. You'll always find the volume (75cl for a standard bottle) and the alcohol level – this varies quite a lot, from under, say, 9% for some light whites, to 14% or more for richer styles of table wine, so it's really worth checking out. The country of origin should be clear too, and the region, either small (Barossa Valley) or large (South-Eastern Australia), depending on how wide an area the fruit came from. The producer's name will be there, and/or a winery or brand name, like Château de Sours (a Bordeaux chateau), Villa Maria (a New Zealand winery) or Jacob's Creek (an Australian brand). Be aware that on most bottles from New World countries the grape(s) will be spelt out on the label, but don't expect this in some parts of Europe. France, in particular, tends to display more about the area than about the grapes used, although the Alsace region and the Languedoc in southern France buck this trend. A good back label (and there are plenty of useless ones!) should give you extra info on where and how the wine was made (the climate, the soils, the use of oak, etc.) and indicate the style to expect, also advising on food matches. So a good label should tell you where, when, what, who, how, and how quickly you'll feel the effects of the wine!

Chapter 10
Chile
Featuring Aurelio Montes in Colchagua Valley

Chile's wine regions have a fantastic range of natural resources, so this really is a wonderful place to make wine. You want sunshine for grapes to ripen properly? Chile's got it – warm sunshine but not the sort of scorching heat that might lead to jammy, over-cooked flavours. Very hot weather is kept at bay by two factors affecting this long, thin country: from the west, fresh afternoon breezes blowing off the nearby Pacific Ocean; and from the east, cold air falling down from the Andes mountains at night.

This means the grapes ripen slowly, taking on intense flavours and aromas. Chile's climate often seems to coax just the right amount of ripe, juicy flavours out of the grapes – a rich, bright, fruity personality and deep colour are the hallmarks of Chile's red wines, while freshness and good balance are in all its best whites. Indeed, if you want a good example of all those fruit-salad flavours experts say you can taste in wine, then get stuck into some Chilean bottles, as they really sing out with pure ripe blackcurrant (Cabernet), plum (Merlot) and tropical fruits (Chardonnay). No other country, save perhaps New Zealand, makes such wonderfully fruity wines!

So the climate helps, but what about good soils? Chile's got that too – its key vineyards lie mainly in the middle of the country, to the north and south of the capital Santiago, in valleys between the Andes range and the Pacific coast. Here the vineyards are well protected, with good drainage in the soil of the lower, flatter plains and limestone-rich soils higher up the slopes, which can contribute to more complex flavours in the best wines.

What about that other vital factor – water? In most years, enough rain falls in the winter months, but if there is a shortage of water, then there's the alternative of melting water from the nearby Andes. Chilean winemakers are experts at 'drip' irrigation – the slow, controlled drip-drip system of watering their vines to give exactly the right amount of water to each vineyard every time. They sometimes hold back a bit on the amount of water a vine needs, because (as we've learned in other regions) by 'stressing' the plant they get a smaller crop of deeply flavoured grapes. Other countries practise this method of watering too, but for the Chileans, irrigation is a fine art.

It often surprises people to learn that most of the world's vines are grafted plants – new plants are literally 'stuck' to grow on top of a pest-resistant, foreign older rootstock. This is because the vine-pest phylloxera causes huge damage to vines and in most parts of the world grafting is the only way to prevent its attack. In Chile, phylloxera doesn't exist, so the vines are on their own natural rootstock, which, some argue, can produce better vines that grow more slowly and live longer. On top of that, Chile has many old vines, and ancient vines produce the most characterful, intensely flavoured grapes.

In fact, Chile's vineyards are renowned for their all-round healthy state – the humidity levels are low thanks to those cooling breezes, and the high levels of bright sunlight also helps keep rot down. This means plenty of Chilean winemakers have chosen to go organic – their vineyards are often free of the fungicide, herbicide and pesticide sprays that some vines are treated with. Some of the world's most exciting organic wines have been made in Chile, which seems to turn more 'green' with each vintage!

Chile has, in many ways, made the most of its assets, carving out a niche with good-value, fruity wines, typically very juicy, rounded and soft in style. Indeed, if you have around £5 to spend on a bottle of wine and want upfront, no-nonsense, clean, fresh fruit, Chile really is the place to go. In the past couple of years, we've started to see great-value at around £7 too, and our Wine Club experts are convinced this country is clearly starting to move upmarket in the 21st century.

But Chile has struggled harder to wow the critics at the very top end. Its premium wines used to lack greatness – they remained fun, fruity and a bit simple. Now the most ambitious winemakers are fighting back with some top releases – expensive reds, mainly, that are designed to take on the best from Europe, Australia and the rest of the world. Some of these are indeed show-stoppers and look set to prove that Chile has the potential to make world-beating wine, but it's early days yet for the country's top wines.

For now, Chile remains a source of great-value wine. Our featured red in this chapter is a brilliant example of this – not a real cheapie, but certainly offering bags and bags of rich ripe fruit flavour for the money. It's a Cabernet Sauvignon, and many would say that Cabernet is Chile's signature wine. Chilean Cabernet has such a distinctive blackcurrant lushness that it sometimes seems like a concentrated essence of this grape variety!

Red blends haven't always played a big part here. Although some of their top-notch 'icon' wines are blends and more look set to appear in the future, for now you'll see more single-variety wines. So, let's look at the other two key Chilean red grapes: Merlot and Carmenère. Carmen-what? There's an interesting story here. The Chileans discovered in 1994 that much of what they thought was Merlot in their vineyards was, in fact, a quite different grape variety, the more obscure Carmenère. Now they've decided it makes rather good wine, thank you very much, so they are putting it out under its own name and taking better care of it in the vineyards. Interestingly, it looks like Carmenère was transported from Bordeaux

JOE WADSACK'S EXPERT TIP

Avoiding Bar Snacks
This is less of a tip, more a piece of advice. Some bar snacks can have connotations on the rest of the evening, particularly high-fat nuts. With gin and tonics they are fine, but never ever ever put peanuts or macadamia nuts out for guests to accompany wine before a meal. Nuts like these are so high in fat content that they simply 'Scotchguard' your tongue. The wine or fizz that you're then trying to taste just runs off the impermeable layer of oil that sticks to the surface of tongue. As a professional taster, I will not eat peanuts up to 24 hours before a tasting. From my experience you are best sticking to other snacks, such as rice crackers, plain salted crisps (flavoured ones are often smothered in sugar which makes wine taste mean and thin) and fresh canapés. As far as other nuts go, roasted almonds are OK, and actually taste quite delicious with high acid wines like Champagne. Remember, the finer, more complex and delicate the wine, the worse the effect that fatty snacks will have.

in the late 19th century, and it would appear to have thrived better in Chile than in France! It still tastes quite a lot like Merlot, but has a slightly more savoury character. Merlot here can be wonderfully juicy, bursting with raspberry and plum and sometimes enhanced by some spicy wood. Joyful stuff!

Pinot Noir makes a few worthwhile and (yet again) good-value reds in Chile, especially in the cool Casablanca region. Whites are mainly represented by easy-going, tangy Chardonnays, some bigger and oakier than others, and aromatic Sauvignon Blancs, although look out for occasional Semillons, Rieslings, Gewurztraminers and Viogniers too. In fact, make a point of searching these other varieties out, because the last thing you want is to get stuck into a rut of simply trying Chile's Chardonnays and overlooking the exciting whites they make from other grapes.

There's a strong sense of 'old meets new' in Chilean wineries. The industry is a sophisticated, surprisingly formal one. Some of the oldest wine estates boast handsome manor houses behind wrought-iron gates, with stunning landscaped gardens. Several historic companies have managed to keep up with the times in the vineyards and wineries, but maintain a traditional image – you can see that in some of the European-style elegant labels. And several have joined up with international consultants, especially French ones, to help create their wines. Some of the world's top winemakers have worked with Chilean wineries – the link with American investment is strong too. Now the trend is back towards home-grown talent, with some dynamic young Chileans – men and women – at work in the top wineries.

The key regions to know about are: Aconcagua Valley, which is historically important as an area for Cabernet Sauvignon; Casablanca Valley, near the coast, has a

SUSY ATKINS' EXPERT TIP

Ordering Wines for Weddings and Functions
People tend to get in a real sweat when they're ordering wine for big parties, especially weddings. Don't stress out – just follow a few simple rules and your bottles will be brilliant. First, always taste before you buy. Never commit to buying wine in bulk unless you have had a proper chance to sit down and decide if you like it. Insist on tasting the wine you intend to buy from a merchant, or ask the venue where your function will be to taste the wines from their list before you commit. You should be given a free tasting, but if you're not, vote with your feet and spend your money elsewhere. If you are planning to get wine from a supermarket, buy a few bottles (or half-bottles) and hold a mini-tasting at home to see which ones you and your family prefer. Avoid wines with 'difficult' characteristics – too oaky, too tannic, too tart or too sweet. Once you've decided on the wine, purchase it from somewhere that will let you have it on a 'sale or return' basis so you can take back what isn't used up and get your money back. Then you can buy lots and lots of it without worrying about waste – it's no good running out of booze in the middle of a big, special occasion!

particularly cool climate and makes some of Chile's most subtle and elegant white wines, mainly Sauvignon Blanc and Chardonnay. The Central Valley is divided into four regions: Maipo, where many traditional wineries are based, makes some superb red wines, especially Cabernets; Rapel is sub-divided into Cachapoal and Colchagua, and both are famous for reds made from Cabernet, Syrah, Merlot and especially Carmenère; Curico turns out lots of good-value wine, both red and white; and the huge Maule area makes some of the least expensive, easy-drinking, mass-produced styles. To the south and north of these main regions are some newer spots where vines are being developed: Bio-Bio to the south is especially exciting for fresh whites, while Limari, five hours' drive north of Santiago and close to the Atacama desert, is newly acclaimed for Chardonnay and Syrah.

Grower Profile Aurelio Montes

**Most of the best modern winemakers are great travellers.
As well as knowing their own region like the back of their hand,
they jet off to other wine countries, picking up and exchanging
ideas all the time, taking home new developments and techniques.
Aurelio Montes is one of the most dedicated travellers – although
he is clearly devoted to Chile and Chilean wine, he has made it
an essential part of his job to roam the globe, meeting other
winemakers and broadening his horizons.**

He happily admits French, Australian and Californian wines have
been major influences on his work, and he is now a sought-after judge
at international wine competitions. 'It's very important to be exposed
to other New World wine countries, and also to the modern methods
appearing in Old World wines,' he believes. 'I'm deeply proud of my
Chilean heritage, but the knowledge gained from years of travel, study
and experimentation has been key to my work.'

He channels all this experience back into the Montes winery, making
it one of the most high-tech and impressive in Chile. Founded in 1988,
Montes is one of the top estates in the modern era of Chilean winemaking.
Aurelio says: 'As a Chilean, I've been very fortunate to experience such
an important period in wine here – the development has been amazing.

Winemakers here used to be mere employees, who had little or no leeway, but in the last fifteen years we have been able to experiment, head in new directions and change our equipment from dated to state of the art. It's a very exciting time to be a winemaker in Chile!'

He thinks it's essential that Chile aims for quality rather than quantity. To this end, he has been a leader in Chile's push towards premium wine production – as well as working at Montes, Aurelio acts as consultant at several other Chilean wineries, even ones that are in direct competition with his own! 'We're having fun in this country,' he says, 'finding exactly the right places for vineyards, such as cooler areas for whites and warmer ones for reds, or planting high up on hillside slopes for different flavours . . . we're getting better at this all the time and I'm really optimistic for the future.'

Born in Santiago in 1948, Aurelio Montes studied oenology at the Catholic University there and then completed his military service. After that, he was off, flying round the globe learning about wine in different countries. Once home, he worked for two prominent wineries in Chile before getting together with three partners to found Montes in 1988.

The team was among the first in Chile to experiment with low-yielding vines (for more concentration and flavour), as well as pioneering the use of French oak barrels and planting at higher altitudes. Aurelio and his partners decreed that the winery would create only a premium range of wines, turning their backs on anything cheap or bulk-produced. Since then, Montes has won several gold medals in a range of international competitions, and in 1995, Aurelio was recognised by his peers and named Chilean Winemaker of the Year by the Chilean Association of Oenologists.

Montes' key vineyards are in the Colchagua Valley, an area with deep loamy soils, abundant water supplies, and plenty of fresh, dry, sunny weather, with the cool nights that are key to the

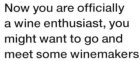

JEAN-MARC SAUBOUA'S EXPERT TIP

Wine Jargon
Now you are officially a wine enthusiast, you might want to go and meet some winemakers at their vineyards, but if you want to follow the conversation you'll need to remember a few key words from the grower's jargon. 'Fruit' will be grapes; 'body' is the weight of the wine conveyed by its flavour and alcohol; 'acidity' gives freshness – without acidity wine would be flat and flabby, with too much it would taste green and sharp; 'fat wine' has flavour and texture that fills the mouth. 'Fermentation' is the conversion of grape juice to alcohol; 'must' is unfermented grape juice; 'malolactic fermentation' is the secondary fermentation that takes place after the alcoholic fermentation – all red wines undergo malolactic fermentation. 'Length' is when flavours and aromas linger after swallowing – the longer the better; 'structure' is the architecture of a wine's body– without structure wine is bland and dull and will not last; 'tannin' is a vital component of red wine, especially wine destined for ageing. So there you are – you can parlé grower!

slow development of flavour in the grapes. Colchagua is especially renowned for its fine red wines. The winery owns La Finca de Apalta here, in the smaller Apalta Valley, one of Colchagua's most exciting sub-zones. Indeed, Aurelio has been credited with putting Apalta firmly on the map. The land here is crescent-shaped and formed mainly by steep slopes, with the vines facing south. Aurelio has discovered that this position gives the fruit a gentle exposure to the hot sun. 'Up on the slopes, the temperature is milder, helping to create a slower yet complete ripening of the grapes,' he says. 'This way, we get more complex, intense flavours in the wine.'

His team opened their impressive new Apalta winery in December 2005. Truly state-of-the-art, it was designed along 'feng shui' principles, ensuring that water, metal, earth and wood are all integrated to help the energy pour into the winery. For example, pools of water and skylights are used to let water and light 'flow' into the building easily. There is also a highly modern emphasis on using gravity to move the wine instead of pumps, using specially designed holes and elevators. Aurelio believes the new winery is the most technically advanced in Chile.

He seems especially fond of two red grapes: Cabernet Sauvignon (our featured wine from Montes), and Syrah (aka Shiraz), which he thinks has a very promising future in Chile. 'The climate here allows us to make reds that are complex, with true fruit expression, but at the same time soft, rounded and velvety, so easy to enjoy,' he says.

'Cabernet has everything you need to make a good wine. Fine structure, fruit, elegance, ageing potential, and so on. I've worked with this grape for so long and I'm convinced it is perfectly adapted to the Chilean soil and climate. I prefer rounded Cabernets, with tannins and good length, but soft and balanced. The oak must be a complement to the fruit and well-integrated.'

It's perhaps no surprise to learn that Aurelio's hobby is flying. He also enjoys sailing, skiing and golf, and has five children to keep him on his toes. Then there are all those visits to overseas wineries to keep up with the international wine scene. But whenever possible, he travels within his own country, taking to the skies at the controls of his own plane. It's easy to picture him scanning the Chilean landscape below for the next site to inspire a Montes vineyard . . .

Grape Variety
Cabernet Sauvignon

We've already met the Cabernet Sauvignon grape in Chapter 3, as one of the grape varieties in our Bordeaux blend. In this chapter it's used on its own to produce a 100% single-variety wine, so it's time for a closer look at the grape and the latest places where it excels.

Cabernet succeeds in lots of different parts of the world, especially the newer wine-producing countries. Chile has particularly high plantings of Cabernet, and it undoubtedly makes some of the country's most exciting red wines. If you can't spot the classic note of blackcurrant in Cabernet Sauvignon, then try a Chilean example, as it simply oozes ripe currants, almost heading into blackcurrant cordial/crème de cassis territory. Some even liken Chilean Cab to black fruit pastilles! You get the picture – blackcurrants, pure, juicy and luscious, are at the core.

Argentina is doing pretty well with Cabernet too, although it tends to be overshadowed by Malbec in this South American country. In the States, Californian Cabernet is considered one of the best wines of all. It can certainly make seriously powerful, full-bodied, complex wines in Napa and Sonoma, which provide great big mouthfuls of flavour and tannin. Australia also makes some blockbusters, particularly in Clare Valley and McLaren Vale, but cooler areas like Yarra Valley and Coonawarra create slightly more elegant, if still intense, wines. South African Cabernet and Cab blends are really worth looking out for – the modern wines show a vast improvement on the tired Cape Cabs of old and have lots of rich cassis and some firm structure.

Tasting Notes Montes Reserve Cabernet Sauvignon

Susy Atkins

'Chile made its name with wines like this – ripe, intensely fruity Cabernets which sing out with pure, rich cassis flavour. It reminds me of blackcurrant pie straight from the oven! Despite being packed with squashy, super-ripe black fruit which lingers long on the palate, it is surprisingly smooth and rounded and easy to enjoy. It's pretty big though, and best with food, especially lamb or beef.'

Joe Wadsack

'The clear quality of fruit in this Chilean Cabernet Sauvignon is so pure that it ticks the box of every wine cliché. Smoother than a snooker baize, and fruitier than Carmen Miranda, this is a gorgeous blackcurranty mouthful, with a sexy coating of vanilla from time in oak barrels. It is a star with all sorts of food. Top of my list would be a rare rack of English lamb.'

Jean-Marc Sauboua

'Excellent balance, with a core of currant, plum and cedary oak that's tightly wound, intense and concentrated. Young dense and vibrant, it can benefit from a short-term cellaring. Toasty oak adds a dimension on the finish. A real Cabernet Sauvignon with some good notes of pencil sharpening ... reminds me of school! Drink now and for up to three years after the vintage.'

Chile is renowned for its Cabernet Sauvignon, a classic old Bordeaux variety, now thriving on old vines that survived the worldwide phylloxera epidemic thanks to the height of the Andes. From Colchagua, widely regarded as Chile's premier red-wine region, this is a soft, smooth, but rich, ripe red, which has spent six months maturing in oak barrels to further round out its succulent tannins. Perfect for drinking now, it will also keep a good year or two.

Wine Style Guide Experiment with Taste

Our featured Chilean Cabernet is in the intensely fruity style, and if you love it, you should certainly try other New World reds with generous, ripe concentration. Why New World? Well, rich reds from newer wine-producing countries seem to have generously juicy, lush ripeness like this wine, although we'll try to find you a few full-bodied reds from Europe that have this as well.

First off, the Montes Reserve is a pretty serious, impressive wine, so forget buying from the bargain basement to find similar styles. Instead, try other premium Chilean reds, as they are more likely to be rich and hearty. Of course, you'll want to try other Cabernets from Chile (pick them from the best regions, such as Maipo, Rapel and Aconcagua) but leave some space in the wine rack for other Chilean gems like top-notch Carmenère and Merlot, too.

Give the top Argentinian reds a whirl – not only the Cabernets, which can be impressive, but the cherryish, dense but smooth Malbecs (see page 302) and the Syrahs. And Uruguay now makes a chunky, firm red of its own, too, from the rare Tannat grape, so complete your tour of South America's biggest reds with a sip of that, although you will probably find Tannat more tannic!

Then it's north to the United States – California Cabernets are a must, in particular the concentrated, blackcurranty Cabs of Napa Valley. Bordeaux-inspired Californian blends of Cabernet and Merlot (and perhaps some other grapes) are worth a taste, but even better are the most serious, intense

Zinfandels. Top red 'Zin', which has a big heart of raspberry fruit and a sprinkle of black pepper, should really appeal to fans of our featured Chilean Cabernet.

Your next port of call should be Australia. Although Shiraz is the first love of most Aussie winemakers, Cabernet runs it a close second. Try Cabs from Coonawarra for complexity and restraint; Margaret River for a Bordeaux-style blend with Merlot; McLaren Vale for honest, rich, satisfying flavours; and Yarra Valley for an elegant take. Don't miss Cabernet–Shiraz blends too. To be honest, you can go wild with Aussie reds – many of them are in the big, fruity and ripe style, although avoid the real cheapies as they may just taste jammy and sweet, lacking the intense cassis flavour that you love about our Chilean Cab.

New Zealand makes a few chunky reds in the warmer vineyard regions – Hawke's Bay is the best bet for a selection of Cabernet blends, Syrahs and Merlots with the required big fruit flavours and lingering finish. But you'll be spoilt for choice in South Africa. The Cape crusaders are brilliant at luscious reds that burst with succulent berry fruit – try a Cabernet or Cabernet blend before you go any further, and make it one from Stellenbosch or Paarl for the most impressive bottles of all. Then be sure to crack open a premium Pinotage with a barbie one day – top South African Pinotage has plenty of red-berry fruit and (usually) a fine veneer of firm oak too. You can try South African Shiraz for more lush, black-fruit flavours and plenty of depth.

As for European wines, refer to chapter three for lots of info on French Cabernet and Merlot. If you liked our Chilean wine a lot, look towards the warm-climate wine-producing regions of Europe for similar styles of ultra-fruity red. That means the south of France, and especially Languedoc (look for Vin de Pays d'Oc reds), Rhône Valley (for whopping great Syrahs and Syrah blends), Sicily (where modern wineries are turning out monster modern reds) and several regions of Spain (the biggest reds of all, with loads of flavour and body, come from Priorato in Catalonia). Pair all big, ripe reds with hearty food, especially roast red meats, mature hard cheeses, warming rich curries and rare steaks.

Shopping for Wine

Time was when wine lovers only ever went to a specialist wine merchant to stock up their cellars. Now we have an amazingly wide range of places to buy our vino – supermarkets, off-licences, mail order, internet and smaller merchants. Be canny and use every option, when and where it suits you best. For example, it's easy to grab the odd bottle in the supermarket along with your food, and prices are competitive there, with a typically fast turnover (so fresher bottles) and often good offers on the big brands in particular. But the off-licence chains and small, independent merchants should be able to give a more interesting, diverse selection, some quirkier 'finds' and a truly personal service, sometimes with free in-store tastings, so they may be better when you have time to browse, chat and fill up the boot! Mail order/internet shopping has the added bonus of your wine arriving conveniently on the doorstep (let's face it, wine is a bulky, heavy and fragile item to haul around) and can provide good case (twelve bottle) offers – but always use a well-established, reputable company who offer a 100% money back guarantee like the Wine Club, so there's no risk experimenting. Our experts' favourite way to buy wine, though, is probably at the cellar door – taking a break in a wine region to tour the wineries, tasting at leisure and picking up a few bottles along the way. Most of us don't have the luxury of doing this very often, but do try occasionally, as there is something special about buying wine in the place where it was made and meeting the people who crafted it!

Chapter 11

California

Featuring the Kautz Family in the Sierra Foothills

Think of California and you'll probably conjure up a vision of sunshine, surf and healthy living. This follows with the image of Californian wine – the preconception is you can almost taste the sunshine in a range of modern, fruity styles with easy-to-understand labels and ripe, summery flavours. So is it really this good?

It's certainly rich and ripe. California doesn't do weedy wine (with the exception of 'blush'/white Zinfandels, the one truly bland style coming out of the state). It excels with blockbuster Cabernets, so chunky and rich you almost need a knife and fork to get into them; creamy-oaky Chardonnays; ripe, ruddy Zinfandels; powerfully fruity fine sparklers; and modern, juicy, deeply coloured rosés.

Even its cheaper wines seem to have a lot of flavour packed into them, but the most inexpensive, accessible Californian wines also sometimes have too much sweetness and oaky flavour. We suggest you steer clear of the 'bargain' Californian wines that hit the UK shelves – this is not a country that does cheap wine very well!

But splash out on the premium wines from California and it's quite a different story. At the top end of the list, California is truly impressive. Its best reds – Cabernets, Merlots, Zinfandels and Pinot Noirs – can take on the famous chateaux of France, and its finest whites (especially the Chardonnays) are excellent, complex creations. Even the luxury sparklers from California are generally reckoned to be worth their rather scary price tags; many think this is the best fizz in the world outside the Champagne region of France. And because they are so packed with full-bodied richness and flavour, most of California's top wines – reds, whites and sparklers – can be aged for years.

You get the picture. At the bottom end, California sends us too much boring, over-blown cheap wine (mainly the big brands), but at the top end it makes the sort of stuff that serious collectors squirrel away in their cellars. Much of it is extremely expensive. In between are some very decent wines that can give the rest of us a taste of premium Californian wine. In fact, it would be good if there were more Cabs, Chardonnays, Merlots and Pinots available around the £8–£12 mark in the UK, because this is where California starts to make a big impression, and where most of us could afford to splash out occasionally and try it!

There are wineries scattered across the United States, and the most important wine regions include Oregon, Washington State and Long Island, near New York City, but California is by far the most important, as it makes 90% of America's wine. Here are some enlightening figures which prove how important this single American state is to the wine world – California makes

around 440 million gallons of wine each year, and is the fourth largest wine 'country' on the planet, behind only Italy, France and Spain. It is home to nearly 1,300 wineries and its wine industry employs 207,000 people. That's some business!

In fact, California's vineyards take up an area larger than Germany, the Netherlands and Belgium combined! Its vines stretch from San Diego near the Mexican border in the south, right up to Mendocino, some 150 kilometres north of San Francisco, and from close to the Pacific Ocean coast, inland across the hot Central Valley to the foothills of the Sierra Nevada mountain range. Within this there are warmer regions, generally the source of the richer reds, and cooler spots where grapes are grown for Pinot Noir, lighter white wines and sparklers.

The state is divided into over 80 AVAs – American Viticultural Areas. The most famous of these are in Napa Valley, just north of San Francisco, and home to some of the most glamorous and wealthy wine estates. Napa is famous for its award-winning, powerful red wines. Just across the Mayacamus mountains from Napa are more AVAs, in the equally renowned Sonoma County. Sonoma makes a wide range of wines, from the great Zinfandels of Dry Creek Valley, to the elegant reds and Chardonnays of Russian River and Sonoma Coast. South of Napa and Sonoma, Carneros is cooler and foggier and makes some of the state's best Pinot Noir, Chardonnay and sparklers.

Up at the northern end of the state, rural, slightly hippy Mendocino has a high proportion of organic vineyards, and some winemakers are converting to the more extreme biodynamics (see page 114 for more

(see page 114 for more

SUSY ATKINS' EXPERT TIP

Fortified Wines

Don't dismiss port, sherry and madeira because they seem old-fashioned! These are great classic drinks from Spain and Portugal and should be appreciated- especially when you need a warming drop of something concentrated and strong. Think chilly nights, log fires, the end of a big feast . . . Fortified wines are a blend of wine with spirit, which stops the fermentation while upping the alcohol levels, leaving a powerful but often sweet concoction. Drink red ports (ruby, late-bottled vintage and vintage ports) after dinner with cheese, or tawny port (oaked aged for a long time for a nutty mellow character) with chocolate puds. The sweetest sherries and madeiras go well with rich cakes and other hearty puddings, with a handful of dried fruits and nuts or an indulgent box of chocs! Alternatively, sip these fortified wines instead of dessert! A little goes a long way, as they taste so intense, so serve in small amounts. That means what sometimes looks like an expensive bottle of fortified wine can turn out to be quite good value as it stretches a long way . . . Dry, pale sherries (these are called finos or manzanillas) are best served well chilled, very fresh and young and partnered with salty nibbles like olives, cured meats, crisps and nuts. Lemony, clean-tasting and almost bracing, dry sherry is one of the most refreshing aperitifs ever. Ask the Spanish, who adore drinking their finest dry sherries in tapas bars, icey cold with a wide range of savoury snacks. Contrary to popular belief fortified wines don't keep for months once opened, but they do keep longer than ordinary table wines – two to three weeks, as a general rule. ❞

on organic and Jean-Marc's take on biodynamic wines). The Central Coast, which stretches from San Francisco to Los Angeles, has a hot inland area which produces much of the cheaper, everyday, simple Californian wines, but there are also cooler climate AVAs on the coast, like Santa Barbara and Monterey. The mountainous Santa Cruz region, south of San Francisco, is where the more maverick producers work, making unusual but bold, striking reds, sometimes with Rhône or Italian varieties. Further south in San Luis Obispo, Edna Valley is responsible for some of the state's most delicious and well-balanced Chardonnays. Finally, the Sierra Foothills vineyards are currently wowing the critics with their rich, hearty reds. Look out for Zinfandel, Syrah and even Sangiovese from here.

Anyone who has seen *Sideways*, the film about two guys on a wine-tasting trip in California, will know that Pinot Noir is considered a 'holy grail' in the state. This red-grape variety is a tricky one, which demands exactly the right conditions before it will produce the silky-smooth, aromatic strawberry character for which it is famous. The Californians are determined to get it right, planting Pinot generally in their cooler vineyards. Some West Coast Pinots are, indeed, quite brilliant, and some think this is the second-best place in the world for the grape (Burgundy in France is its first home); however, the New Zealanders would probably disagree!

Cabernet is just as important in California, and the best examples are thrilling, with big, four-square structure and rich flavours galore. They can age terrifically well, although the 'cult' Cabs of Napa Valley can be – you guessed it – hugely expensive. Some criticism is levelled at the most gigantic styles – it's argued that it's very difficult to drink (rather than taste) such a tannic and concentrated wine. Still, match a fine Napa Cab with steak and the combination works pretty well! Less pricey, less hefty Californian Cabernets are more approachable, with plenty of cassis and plum flavours.

Zinfandel is well worth a try – not the boring, insipid white or blush Zinfandels,

JEAN-MARC SAUBOUA'S EXPERT TIP

Noble Rot

'Noble rot' is a term easily remembered because of the contradictory word association! The great sweet wines such as Sauternes and Trockenbeerenauslese, (like Sergio Mottura's Muffo see the Grower Profile in Chapter 5) are made from grapes attacked by noble rot. But what is it? Well, when humid conditions in the morning are followed by the heat during the rest of the day, the fungus botrytis cinerea can appear in its beneficial form – noble rot or pourriture noble. In this form it results in shrivelled grapes with a very high sugar level. But waiting for noble rot is a risky business: the wrong kind of rot can occur if the weather changes, then the grower loses their whole crop, which is why the wines made this way are more precious. Certain white grapes with thin skins are particularly susceptible to noble rot, and these include Semillon and Riesling. This will make some of the richest wine in the world, developing the most complex aromas of dry apricot and marmalade. A truly seductive wine all the more special because of its "noble" origins!

which are just pale rosés, but the real reds made from this grape, which have loads of sweetly ripe raspberry and bramble flavour, plenty of guts and body and a twist of black pepper on the finish. 'Zin' goes really well with the classic Christmas/Thanksgiving turkey feast. Merlot is not quite as trendy as it was a few years ago, but the most talented winemakers coax lots of gorgeous cherry and plum flavour out of it and can make superb wines to rival Bordeaux. Cheap Californian Merlot can be a bit sweetish, jammy and simple, though.

Fashion counts for a lot in the States, of course, and certain grape varieties have popped in and out of vogue. If Merlot used to be America's most fashionable red grape, Chardonnay was certainly the 'hot' white. And if you like Chardonnay, tasting some fine examples from the West Coast is still a must. But everyday Californian Chardonnays are a bit like everyday Aussie ones – rather uniform, oaky and unexciting, and so its star is slightly on the wane. More hip currently (and making a refreshing change from the norm) are peachy Viognier and 'new-wave' Sauvignon Blanc. New wave? The Americans used to like their Sauvignons oddly oaked and off-dry, in a style they labelled 'Fumé Blanc', but thank goodness they now make plenty in the crisp, zesty style that the UK adores.

When you taste Californian wine, bear in mind the cooler areas (detailed above) will give you more elegant, subtle flavours and crisper acidity, while the warm parts still put out the blockbuster, concentrated wines that made the state famous. Sample a wide range and do give the fine sparklers a try. Once in a while you should even treat yourself to one of the more expensive wines from the state, just to see what some of the world's most talented winemakers are up to. This is one 'country' where it pays to splash out.

JOE WADSACK'S EXPERT TIP

Champagne and Magnums
This is the ultimate purchase tip: All Champagne always tastes better in magnums. They look a whole lot groovier, and they don't cost you a penny more. What's a magnum? It's a double-sized bottle – one and a half litres, in other words, which is considered to be the perfect size to age Champagne. So convinced is the great Champagne house of Bollinger, that all its reserve wine is stored in magnums. That's a hugely labour-intensive and expensive process, so there has to be some truth in it. When I say all Champagne tastes better out of magnums, I do mean all Champagne. Even the least prestigious own-label supermarket Champagnes taste better this size, and here's why: for commercial reasons most, if not all, Champagne is released before its peak, even Bollinger, which is already at least three years old when it's sold in bottle and still tastes a little young. Magnums age more slowly, so they are kept back until they are ready for sale. So, for example, when a magnum of Bollinger is released, it's almost certainly more than six years old. It tastes silkier and smells more divine, yet costs the same as two regular bottles of the three-year-old stuff. And when you take my advice and bring out your magnum of Champagne before midnight on New Year's Eve, who'll be the daddy?

Grower Profile The Kautz Family

Close by the Sierra mountains, in the heart of California's scenic 'Gold Rush' country, lies Ironstone Vineyards, who not only make delicious wines but also have a museum on site which houses the treasures from the gold-panning era. Here you'll find a forty-four pound 'nugget' – officially a 'crystalline gold leaf specimen' – the largest in the world!

The Gold Rush may be over in the Sierra Foothills, but the vineyards and wineries have now created a new rush – wine enthusiasts flocking to the region. Located east of Sacramento and the hot Central Valley, the Sierra Foothills have a strong winemaking heritage; amazingly, there were already one hundred wineries in these hills by the late 19th century. During the Prohibition era, this dwindled to just one, and the vineyards were all but abandoned. Luckily, the land was of such low value that it was not worth pulling many of the vines out, so they lay uncultivated.

The first signs of a winemaking revival came in the late 1960s, when a group of pioneers from Sacramento began purchasing grapes here. Large wineries from outside the area saw the potential in the unique old vineyards, especially the ancient gnarled Zinfandel plants which produce wonderfully concentrated red grapes. The revival of the Sierra Foothills, cooler and more fragmented than the hot Central Valley plains, was under way.

The history of Ironstone Vineyards starts with a young row-crop farmer John Kautz, who in the late 1940s saw the future in growing wine grapes and eventually amassed over 5,000 acres of vines in Lodi and the Sierra Foothills.

John became one of the top-ten grape growers in California and, in 1988, he and his wife Gail decided to make a wine of their own. They continued to grow grapes to sell on, but at the same time they launched Kautz Wines, which evolved into Ironstone Vineyards. The name Ironstone came about after a crew of miners had to blast through incredibly hard rock on the family ranch to create the wine-ageing cellars.

Now at the Ironstone winery, there is a tasting room and gourmet deli, a heritage museum, outdoor amphitheatre, 14 acres of lakeside gardens, that enormous gold nugget, and of course a state-of-the-art winery! There's always something happening here, from wine tasting tours to cookery demos, movies and concerts.

The wines are highly regarded. While much of California's wine industry offers either bottles only at the high, luxury end of the market, or mass-produced big brands, Ironstone aims to make quality wines at a reasonable price for everyday enjoyment. The family's aim for the Ironstone Wines range is that the experience of enjoying wine should not only be for connoisseurs but for everyone from every household. But the 'Reserve' label is the premium range, available in small quantities, only at the winery's tasting room and in fine restaurants.

Ironstone's grapes come from two regions – their prime vineyards in the valley of Lodi, close to the Pacific Ocean coast, and the Sierra Foothills, which has varied soil types and higher altitude. Fruit from both areas is allowed to ripen slowly and evenly to develop intense aromas and flavours. It is eventually blended to provide consistent quality from vintage to vintage.

This is a real family business. John and Gail and each of their four children – Stephen, Kurt, Jack and Joan – are actively involved in the company. 'It makes us very proud that all of our kids work in the business,' says John. 'We are one of the few companies that is 100% family-owned and operated, from the dirt in the ground, to the bottle!'

Joan Kautz-Meier, John's daughter, is Vice-President of International Operations at Ironstone. Despite the rather grand title, she is down-to-earth with an unpretentious enthusiasm for fine wine. 'We served our Cabernet Franc Reserve at my wedding and we make a very nice Chardonnay, Merlot and Cabernet, but I never like to name a particular

wine as my favourite, because what I prefer will be completely different from the next person. That's what makes wine fun!' she says.

During her childhood, Joan remembers being bored rigid, sitting in the car whilst being driven around vineyards as her parents negotiated and met up with wineries to sell their grapes. Joan says she was desperate to play with her friends and couldn't understand what was so interesting about staring out of the window at the constant rows of vines. In fact, it wasn't until her college days that Joan began to appreciate the family winery, and after 'killing every plant I ever owned' and not finding much she enjoyed on her college botany course, Joan decided she was far more interested in the marketing side of the business. This has proved the perfect mix, as her brothers were most interested in the agricultural side of viticulture.

Joan's daughter Madison recently celebrated her first birthday and is regularly in attendance at meetings and accompanies Joan on trips to the winery, vineyards and wine events. Joan jokes that Madison had flown 40,000 miles by the age of one, so is being well groomed to take over the international side of the business! This is typical of the family who combine work and their home lives. Joan's ten-year-old niece already helps out in school holidays, often volunteering to help answer phones and producing an Ironstone newsletter for the staff, containing lots of gossip about what's going on!

Joan thinks the Wine Club's featured Chardonnay–Viognier is great with many foods because it is fairly rich. 'It will be a versatile match for chicken, fish and light pasta. We have a wonderful recipe book here at the winery with barbecued oysters, pan-seared prawns, marinated mussels, Mediterranean tuna salad, sweet potato gnocchi with sage pesto – all these would go great with the Chardonnay–Viognier!'

She is ambitious for the future of Californian wine, but despite its recent success, still feels the Sierra Foothills has a long way to go. 'The diverse varieties and wider price range is incredible here, but there are many people who do not know about it. I would love for them to look outside the best-known regions like Napa and Sonoma and see that there are some other outstanding regions here producing wonderful, well-priced wines. I hope consumers will become more adventurous with Californian wines.'

California is not just about big brands or the same old grape varieties – or indeed about terrifyingly expensive collector's bottles from Napa Valley (although there is something to be said for all these aspects of West Coast wine). At heart, Californian wine is best when it comes from smaller companies that retain something of the pioneer spirit, and who grow their grapes in regions that they know intimately and love. The Kautz family, still grape growers at heart, clearly care for their vineyards in Lodi and the Sierra Foothills very deeply. This is not just big business, American-style.

Joan thinks California is an amazing place all round. 'Everything anyone could want is here. You can literally snow-ski in the morning and water-ski in the afternoon. Between the beaches, the mountains, deserts, cities and country, there is something for everyone.' Including, of course, some terrific wines!

Grape Variety Viognier

We looked closely at the Chardonnay grape in Chapter 2, so here's everything you need to know about Viognier, the white grape that appears in the blend with Chardonnay in our delicious, sunny Californian wine featured in this chapter.

In fact, if you like 100% Chardonnays, you'll almost certainly enjoy Viognier on its own too, as it's roughly in the same style-category of whites – generously fruity, ripe and perfumed with fleshy tropical fruit flavours. But where Chardonnay usually has fruit cocktail notes of oranges, apples and pineapple (among others), Viognier has a very distinctive, more specific and easily identifiable note of peach and apricot.

There's been a lot of talk lately about this variety – Viognier is hugely fashionable at the moment, and has been heralded by some as 'the new Chardonnay'. Top bottles are certainly impressive. The best Viogniers are full-bodied, headily perfumed (think honeysuckle blossom) and packed with rich, peachy flavour, sometimes with a slightly honeyed note on the finish, though dry. Great, then, especially with rich, creamy chicken dishes and mild fruity curries. But be aware there are some less interesting Viogniers around that somehow lack that essential peachy flavour and aroma.

It's simply a case of a winemaker getting the right amount of ripeness and balancing acidity from this grape – and some get it more right than others! Try to find one which has plenty of concentration and character – that is, after all, the point of this variety. The top Viogniers come from the Rhône Valley (Condrieu and Château-Grillet) while there are some good-value wines from the south of France, with a few contenders from California, Australia and Argentina.

Viognier is sometimes used in red blends in the Rhône Valley, where the fragrant white grapes add elegance and perfume; in fact, our Australian growers in Chapter 7 use Viognier with Shiraz. And in our featured wine in this chapter, it makes a lovely fruity blend with Chardonnay, the grape with which it is most often compared.

Tasting Notes Ironstone Chardonnay–Viognier

Susy Atkins

'You can almost taste the sunshine in this bright, vivacious white wine. It's got lots of juicy apricot and pineapple fruit, with a rich, creamy texture and some fresh acidity to balance it out. It's not oaky – there's no spicy-vanilla character here – but it is ripe and lively. Roast a chicken with garlic and lemon and crack this open and you'll have the perfect cheering Sunday lunch!'

Joe Wadsack

'The nose is full of rich tropical fruits like guava and melon, while the juicy nectarine-infused flavours are as silky and as round as Marilyn Monroe's behind. Big, curvy and unctuously proportioned wines like this are terrific with creamy curries and rice dishes like seafood risotto.'

Jean-Marc Sauboua

'Deliciously ripe, wonderfully perfumed, floral aromas come through on the palate as well, with rich fig, apricot and honeyed flavours that are pure and delicious. I love its richness and opulence. A real racy style and a substantial white. Drink now and keep for up to two years from vintage.'

Many Californian Chardonnays are, unsurprisingly, big, rich, buttery wines. The Ironstone is somewhat subtler, with delicate aromas of apricot, orange blossom and citrus leading on to a refined and elegant palate. The crisp melony fruit from the Chardonnay blends wonderfully with the more exotic spicy notes of the Viognier grape – posh Chablis meets posh Condrieu.

FINE WINE OF CALIFORNIA

IRONSTONE
Vineyards

FAMILY SELECTION

2004   2004

BARREL AGED

CHARDONNAY VIOGNIER

Wine Style Guide Experiment with Taste

It's impossible not to like fruity whites – ones which major on very juicy, fruit-salad flavours. Some critics call these wines 'fruit-driven' – the flavours of the orchard, or tropics, are what hit you most, and smelling them is like walking into a greengrocer's shop! Other whites smell grassy, or spicy, or creamily oaky, but these are like the scent on your hands when you have been cutting up ripe, squashy, pulpy fruits.

Viognier is a part of the blend of our featured wine, so the first thing to do is get out and try some single variety Viogniers. If you can splash out on a Condrieu or Château-Grillet from the northern Rhône, then great – these wonderfully concentrated, opulent whites made from Viognier are full-bodied, perfumed and delicious, but they are expensive. Other examples to try might come from the south of France, Argentina, Australia and California. The price tag will definitely be lower for these Viogniers but you won't get quite the same concentration of peachy flavours either; expect a clean, juicy, fruity white, nevertheless.

The best Chardonnays in the fruity, juicy style come from New Zealand, Australia, Chile, South Africa, Sicily, Argentina, California and the south of France. Phew! That's a lot of Chardonnay to choose from, and to be honest, at the cheaper price points, quite a lot of it tastes fairly similar! In particular, for well-balanced, fruit-driven styles go for Chardonnays from New Zealand's Marlborough, Hawke's Bay and Martinborough; Australia's Adelaide Hills and Padthaway regions; and California's Sonoma and Carneros.

Try Chardonnay–Semillon blends from Australia, too, for easy-drinking, tropical-fruit-salad whites. You might sample the Sauvignon-Semillon blends from Western Australia, for more fruity flavours. While Down Under, be sure you don't miss the zesty Australian Rieslings, which really do sing out with bright, limey citrus notes.

European Rieslings tend to be a bit too elegant and light to be likened to our starting point, the Californian blend. But the whites of Alsace, in eastern France, are well worth a foray, including the Rieslings, which can be weighty and full, the spicier Gewurztraminers and especially the Tokay–Pinot Gris, which has ripe, almost smokey, peachy fruit. Anyone investigating interesting white wines must make a stop in Alsace!

Sauvignon Blanc from cooler climates also taste too crisp and grassy to compare with this style of fruity white, but from Chile, South Africa, and especially New Zealand you get a big blast of ripe gooseberry flavour, so do explore this avenue. The other grape you must try is Chenin Blanc, which makes wines with an apple-core flavour. Chenin Blanc is made in two parts of the winemaking globe, France's Loire Valley, where the variety creates an amazing range of styles from bone-dry to sticky-sweet and even sparkling. Pick dry or off-dry Vouvray for a taste of fruity French whites, and then track down Chenin Blanc from South Africa, where the best makers are squeezing plenty of apple, lime and guava flavour out of the grapes, making quite a simple, but crowd-pleasing, fruit-driven white that we bet you'll enjoy.

Whites which major on bright, tangy fruit flavour should be matched with flavour-packed, fairly rich fish, chicken and vegetable dishes. Good examples of the perfect partners for this style of wine are: fish in creamy sauces, roast or grilled chicken; mild curries, especially kormas; curries with fruit such as raisins and apricots; fresh salmon steaks; chicken tagines; pasta with creamy seafood sauces; and roasted herby vegetables.

Host a Wine Tasting at Home

It's fun, inspiring and sociable to taste wine with your mates – and comparing the wines always makes for good conversation, if not heated debate! More and more people are planning wine evenings at home – it doesn't have to be complicated. Get each person to bring a bottle, perhaps on a general theme so you can concentrate on one particular region or grape variety, style or price point. If you taste the wines 'blind' it means you will approach every one with a completely open mind – and that can lead to some surprises, as you discover perhaps you do like German Riesling after all! Get everyone to wrap the bottles up in silver foil beforehand and remove the plastic or lead capsule from the top too, as that sometimes gives the brand or region away. Then taste each bottle in turn, revealing all the labels – and prices – only at the end of the session. If you've tasted the wines of one particular country, why not plan a supper around that country too, so you can enjoy drinking your favourite bottle with some great food once the tasting is over? Some people might like to take notes on the wines, and why not? This is a very good way of keeping a record of the best/worst bottles of the night. It can be easy to forget what you've enjoyed during the evening, and you do want to learn from the experience as well as have fun!

Chapter 12
Argentina
Featuring José Alberto Zuccardi in Mendoza

Of all the new wine countries we've profiled, Argentina is probably the least well-known. In fact, it is likely most of our Wine Club members hadn't even tasted an Argentinian wine until we featured the Zuccardi Malbec. Argentina's wine is a fairly new arrival on the UK shop shelves, but for reasons we shall discover, it is one of the most exciting, up-and-coming new sources of wine in the world.

New? Well, not exactly. Argentina's first vineyards were established in 1557! And it is certainly not a small producer – in volume terms, the country is the fifth largest in the world and the second largest 'New World' wine country. So it's not exactly a minor producer . . .

But until recently the local population lapped up most of its own vino. Export to overseas markets like the UK started relatively late and it was only after the disastrous collapse of its economy in 2001 that Argentina realised it had to put a huge effort into selling its wines abroad. Now you'll see wine from this country all over our shops, and much of it is very good value for money.

Argentina stretches down the southern-most tip of the Americas. It has mountains and plains, lush green forests and deserts, dramatic waterfalls and glaciers. Unsurprisingly, such a wide range of eco-systems includes a number of regions that are suitable for grape growing. The main wine-producing zone is to the west of the country, running from north to south between parallels 22 and 42: there are 210,000 hectares of vines.

So, the Argentinians have vast areas of vineyard, and parts of the country where the climate and soil are great for wine grapes. Like the Chileans, in some areas they can irrigate their vines conveniently with melted snow from the Andes mountains, which form a dramatic backdrop to many vineyards. They have something else too – a really important asset in a newer wine-producing nation. Back in the early 1900s, many immigrant families from winemaking areas of Europe arrived here, bringing samples of their favourite vines with them. This means that today, Argentina has a treasure-trove of superb old vines across a wide range of grape varieties. It has, for example, lots of mature French grapes like

JEAN-MARC SAUBOUA'S EXPERT TIP

Learning Aromas
I love memories. Have you ever wondered why a certain smell will evoke distant memories? This is simply because in your brain the memory or temporal lobe sits just behind the olfactory bulb, which processes messages about an aroma. Vapour rises through the nostrils and from behind the soft palate, into the upper part of the nasal cavity. It then carries the aroma messages along fine nerves to the olfactory bulb. Thus you connect events with certain aromas . . . sounds complicated? Associating wine aromas with memories helps experts fix on grapes and vintages, so, just smell your glass again and close your eyes.

Malbec, Merlot and Syrah, it has the Spanish grape Tempranillo, and a host of Italian varieties including Sangiovese and Barbera. Although it should be added that some lesser-known, inferior grapes are there too, these are hardly ever used for exported wine.

So the most interesting aspect of Argentinian wine is its sheer range. Sure, lots of Chardonnay and Cabernet is grown there, as it is all over the New World, but dig deeper into Argentina's store of fascinating grapes and you will find a diverse range of inspiring flavours to try. Fancy an aromatic white with spicy notes and a refreshing crisp streak? Go for an Argentinian Torrontes (the variety originated in north-west Spain, but is more famous from Argentina now). Or are you aching to see how the lovely Italian grape Barbera fares overseas? Perhaps you want a rich red made from the somewhat obscure French grape Malbec?

Ah, Malbec. This is Argentina's signature grape, and the one you should plump for above all others. Malbec may be French and associated originally with Bordeaux and Cahors, but to many wine lovers it is now synonymous with good, honest, ripe, concentrated South American red. The Argentinians have made a true star out of Malbec, something the French have never done. In some ways, the Malbec of this country is its vinous 'calling card' – a bit like Sauvignon Blanc in New Zealand, and Shiraz in Australia. You haven't discovered Argentinian wine – or, some might argue, New World wine – until you've cracked open a Malbec from the Mendoza region of this country – see the grape variety section on page 302 for lots more info on Malbec.

Although Malbec is the stellar red grape of Argentina, Cabernet Sauvignon comes a close second. Many of the top wineries have great faith in the future for Argentinian Cabernet and have been planting it like crazy in recent years. The results can be pretty good,

JOE WADSACK'S EXPERT TIP

Planning Ahead
The pleasure derived from a delicious glass of wine with friends is infinitely heightened by the anticipation of the experience. An English university proved that the longer you have to wait for a punchline, the funnier you will find the joke. All sensual experiences are improved by a little emotional foreplay, so to speak. Over 90% of wine is consumed within twelve hours of purchase. Imagine how much more fun you would have if you disciplined yourself never to drink a new bottle of wine unless you kept it for at least a week. Trust me, it works. Think of the anticipation that you get from keeping special bottles for the Christmas lunch. They add to the sense of occasion and rarely disappoint. Buying in advance will also save you money. There tend to be many deals on after the wedding season and before the Christmas rush, so it's worth buying a carton of your favourite before the price goes up. Let's face it, you're going to buy them anyway. Classic wines, like Bordeaux, Burgundy and Champagne, if you spend over a tenner on them, will invariably taste better six months later. They are made that way.

too – either Cab on its own or blended with Malbec. Bonarda is the other signature Argentinian red – it's widely planted and makes juicy, light, easy-drinking red. Bonarda is fine if you like a simple, quaffing wine now and again, but don't expect anything like the complexity of the best Malbecs.

Other red grapes to focus on are Syrah (aka Shiraz), which seems to taste especially leathery and spicy from Argentina, Merlot, Tempranillo and Sangiovese. Pinot Noir is being planted in cooler spots, mainly as an experiment.

You must try Torrontes, especially if you like aromatic, dry white wines, and they make a great match with Thai food! Top bottles (always new vintages, as this wine does not keep well) have a crisp, fresh streak and melony, grapey aroma, but be warned – some weak and uninteresting labels do lurk out there, so you may need to try one or two to find a gem. Chardonnay, especially the buttery-oaky style, is popular and reliable, and Sauvignon Blanc is currently in vogue among the country's winemakers, who are coming up with a few refreshing, lively whites. Similarly, there are some promising, good-value sparklers, so we may see more Sauvignons and bubblies from this country in the future.

The most important wine region by far is Mendoza, to the west, right across the country near the Andes mountains and the Chilean border. Mendoza City itself is a delightful place, with attractive old buildings, stone irrigation channels along tree-lined streets and some good Italianate restaurants (many immigrants here came from Italy). The area around the city makes nearly three-quarters of Argentina's wine. The Upper Mendoza River area is one of the best places of all, and includes the sub-zone of Lujan de Cuyo, where some centuries-old vines continue to be harvested.

Still within Mendoza, Maipu is another important site for Malbec, and the Uco Valley, 100 kilometres south, is a new and exciting area under development. Outside Mendoza, the wine regions are far-flung. Among them, 1000 kilometres north of Mendoza city is Salta, a region with notably cool night-time temperatures but high UV rays by day to ripen the fruit – these conditions create intense flavours and aromas in the grapes. Torrontes is at its best from Salta.

Then there's Rio Negro, on the edge of Patagonia, to the far south of the country, where arid desert land has been planted and flourishes,

thanks to water from a large river diversion. Now Rio Negro is producing ripe sunny reds from Malbec, Merlot and Syrah, and some of the best Chardonnays in the country.

So is everything really that bright and optimistic in Argentina's wineries? Certainly it's an exciting time in the development of new wine regions, vineyards, varieties and styles here. But don't expect everything to be perfect – some of the cheaper Chardonnays, Cabernets and Merlots can be a bit uniform, like identikit versions of Australian and Chilean wines. And Argentina needs more 'flagship' wines – bottles at the very top end competing with the best from around the world. Critics tend to complain that, at the moment, they haven't seen enough wines made from the internationally known varieties like Chardonnay and Cabernet with a distinctive character on them, a personality that could be summed up as typically 'Argentinian'.

Nevertheless, Argentina is moving forward admirably, already a producer of sunny, flavoursome and reliable wines, with everything to play for in the future. Those Malbecs (and, to some extent, Torrontes) are undeniably the most interesting bottles of all and the ones which already show a unique Argentinian character. Taste them before you try anything else from Argentina and do keep an eye on this dynamic wine country in the future!

Grower Profile José Alberto Zuccardi

José Alberto Zuccardi is one of the most interesting 'modernisers' we've met, a true 21st-century winemaker. He's a personable, laid-back character, famous for his big smile and quiet charm, but underneath he's incredibly dynamic – there is always a new plan to act out, a new technique to try, a new vineyard to plant and tend. This means that Familia Zuccardi is one of the most progressive and exciting wineries in South America.

The Zuccardi family arrived in Argentina from Avelino in the south of Italy in the late 19th century. In the 1950s, José Alberto's father, Don Alberto, started his own irrigation company in the key wine region of Mendoza, in the foothills of the Andes mountain range. In the rainy UK, it can be hard to understand how important irrigation is to the Argentinians – few crops grow well without it, and the clever use of water from the Andean mountains is worth a fortune to farmers.

In 1963, Don Alberto came up with a great way to demonstrate how good his new irrigation techniques were – he planted vines and irrigated them so they thrived. Inadvertently, a wine company was born. The first vineyard was 16 hectares of land close to Mendoza City. A decade later, to underline his point, he planted a second vineyard in the unforgiving, scrubby Santa Rosa desert half an hour out of Mendoza. Today, his first vineyard has been expanded to ten times its original size, while the dry dust of his original desert plot now holds a verdant 440 hectares of vines!

Don Alberto is a sprightly octogenarian, yet he still visits the family vineyards each week. He never stops searching for new ways to put the company ahead, and keeps up to date with all the latest advances. He's renowned for plucking off all surplus vine leaves or bunches within his reach whenever he's in the vineyard – this method of canopy management (exposing a few bunches of grapes to more sunlight) is considered a family trait and one of the secrets of their success!

José Alberto, Don Alberto's son, has managed the company since 1985. Familia Zuccardi had become well-established as a wine producer by this time, and it remains one of the country's most important wineries – run 'as a family, by a family', as José puts it. In many cases, whole local families are employed by the Zuccardis, and they have been since the vineyards were first planted. 'I believe that good wines are created by good people in healthy vineyards,' he says, 'and that's why I try to give as much responsibility as possible to the families that work for us.'

Labour is relatively cheap and plentiful in Argentina, and it would be easy for a cynical company to take advantage of this. But Familia Zuccardi educates its workers' children in a school they built with the local government and the local farmers. The school now has two hundred pupils and a football pitch! 'We must teach the kids the legendary art of punching a ball into the back of an English net!' laughs José Alberto. Evening classes are offered to workers who want to improve their literacy and numerical skills and they've created a 'cultural centre' in the Santa Rosa vineyards with a library for the workers' use.

José Alberto believes it's important to help workers with accommodation, transport and even basics like winter clothes, shoes and the bicycles which many of them use to get around the vineyards. 'The most important way to make sure they can work hard is to give them a full stomach!' he says. 'So we have a free lunch for all vineyard workers in the canteen.' José Alberto clearly believes he has a responsibility to look after his workers, a refreshing attitude.

The family care for the environment and have been working on a project to turn all their vineyards organic since 1998. This means halting the use of all chemical sprays and artificial fertilisers. The first Zuccardi vineyards were certified organic in 2001 and to date 300 hectares have made the transition. 'We have always believed working with nature is the way to produce wines of quality, character

and appeal,' says José Alberto. 'Our organic vineyards now act as a playground for numerous insects and birds.'

The Zuccardi vines look different from the norm in another key way – the company has plumped for an unusual system of training the vines high up and overhead into pretty, bright green arches. This way of growing vines was brought as an idea from Europe in the late 19th century, but many wineries have moved away from it, considering it old-fashioned. The ever-innovative Zuccardis have kept and adapted the method: the vines are pruned back hard and the tendrils spread out more widely than usual to expose the fruit more fully to the sun. José Alberto believes training the vines up high ventilates them well and protects them from disease and rot.

He looks beyond the obvious in many ways. Take irrigation – most grape growers are now moving away from flood irrigation, which is used to immerse the roots, towards the gentle, slow-drip method. José Alberto is convinced that flood irrigation is, in fact, the best method, as it allows the nutrients in the soil to spread out more evenly. With his family's irrigation background he probably knows what's right!

When hail strikes the Mendoza vineyards, it can be devastating, with ice balls the size of a child's fist, which strip every leaf and bud from the vine. The Zuccardis have an uncompromising approach to protecting their vines, and simply cover the vineyards with massive nylon nets strung above the plants. It costs around $6,500 per hectare to net the vines and so far they've covered almost 60% of their plants, yet another Zuccardi initiative!

The modern, dynamic approach to viticulture is most evident in the sheer range of wines produced at Familia Zuccardi. Of course, Malbec is among the most important varieties grown here: 'It's our emblematic Argentinian variety,' says José Alberto,

SUSY ATKINS' EXPERT TIP

Bottle Sizes
Size matters! When you're throwing a dinner party, it's impressive to bring out magnums of wine or Champagne, as Joe says in the last chapter. A magnum is two ordinary bottles' worth – 1.5 litres in all – and it rarely costs much more than two 75cl bottles. A bigger bottle looks great though – there's something wonderfully generous and impressive about a magnum, let alone a jeroboam, which contains 4.5 litres, or a methuselah which contains 6! Independent wine merchants often have more wines available in magnums than you will find on the high street or in the supermarkets, so go and track down something huge when you're sure you'll get through it.

At the other extreme, try buying wines in half-bottles when you might not finish the bottle quickly, as it means you will open a fresh, new bottle sooner. Halves are especially sensible for concentrated flavours that are often only sipped in small amounts, like dry sherry or dessert wine. These wines need drinking up, not tucking away until they become oxidised and tired, so buy them in smaller bottles and crack open another next time.

'and we were one of the first to make a high quality wine from it.'
But as well as Malbec, this company uses numerous other grape
varieties – Viognier, Tempranillo, Bonarda, Syrah and Zinfandel.
Now their special 'Innovation' project at the winery has an amazing
thirty-five new grape varieties on trial. These include Gamay (the
grape behind Beaujolais), Marsanne, Mourvèdre, Pinot Bianco and
Tannat. These varieties will all be thoroughly assessed for their quality
and suitability for future wines the uncompromising Zuccardi way.

José Alberto identifies four main objectives for his family winery:
'Quality, innovation, the environment and to be useful to the community.'
He appears to be making great strides forward on all counts.

Grape Variety
Malbec

Malbec's orginal home is France, where it is a minor grape in Bordeaux, and the main variety behind the rich, tannic reds of Cahors, in the deeper south-west. It used to be fairly obscure – only serious Francophiles had heard of it. But in the past decade or so, it has become famous as Argentina's signature red.

Malbec vines were brought over by French immigrants, and it is now the most widely planted red grape in Argentina. Most experts believe the variety makes more generously fruity, lush and concentrated red wines in Argentina than in France. Expect a rich core of black-cherry fruit with red plum, cassis and chocolate somewhere in there too, and an intensely juicy, luscious, but fairly smooth, rounded style. Some Malbecs are easy-going and fairly light, while others are fuller and oakier, even quite serious with a leathery, gamey edge and good ageing potential, especially when made from the concentrated fruit of very old vines. Either way, that ripe, juicy black-cherry flavour is a giveaway almost every time. It is widely planted in Mendoza, but some particularly good examples come from the old vines in Lujan de Cuyo and the Salta region.

It is a wonderful red to serve with rare, lean steak – a glorious wine and food marriage that is very often served up in the restaurants of Mendoza and Buenos Aires. It also goes really well with . . . chocolate cake! Yes, we were surprised too, but try it sometime, as the almost sweetly-ripe flavours of this red work a treat with almost anything chocolatey, but especially cake!

Tasting Notes Santa Julia Reserve Malbec

Susy Atkins

'This is an appealing, straightforward, medium-bodied Malbec with black cherry and plum fruit and a fresh note of juicy strawberry. There's a hint of plum pudding too, a spicy, clove note underlying the fruit. It's ripe and generous, smooth and slips down easily! My perfect match for this would be steak frites and salad, or use it as a party red with a buffet . . .'

Joe Wadsack

'Malbec always reminds me of fruitcake and this one is no exception. A nose of dried fruits and caramel, with a spicy, almost strawberry fruit flavour. You can also taste the warmth of the Argentinian sunshine in this wine, with gutsy, savoury, almost leathery notes. Drink with a chargrilled steak or slow-roasted pork.'

Jean-Marc Sauboua

'Flamboyant, mouth-filling and powerful, this is a solid and modern style with dark currant and blackberry fruit riding along cocoa, toast and cedar notes. Ample structure runs through the chocolate finish. The long seamless finish shows depth. Enjoyable now, but this will improve and develop in the bottle over the next two years.'

The Malbec grape flourishes under a hot South American sun, producing wines of real ripeness and softness. The Zuccardi family have produced a sumptuous, blackberry and plummy, fruit-driven wine with soft, oaky vanilla undertones thanks to its ten months careful barrel ageing. Delicious straight away, but it also has the Malbec dual purpose, as it will mature further for four to five years after vintage, giving a different tasting experience later on.

Wine Style Guide Experiment with Taste

Our featured Malbec has lots of very ripe black fruit and a spicy, toasty note. If you like this wine, we bet you enjoyed it most of all with food. This could be an easy-going, ripe party red, but, even better, a great match for steak, roast lamb, rich roast vegetables with herbs and garlic, or a sensational cheeseboard . . .

There are plenty of similar styles of hearty red which will appeal in the same way. Firstly, don't expect all Malbecs to taste like this, as some are lighter and others richer, but do try others. Then taste your way round Argentina's other important reds. That means Malbecs from other regions of the country – try Salta or Lujan de Cuyo or Rio Negro, and the excellent Cabernets and Syrahs that are now appearing more and more. Try Bonarda, too, and compare it with Malbec, as this is Argentina's other speciality red grape. You might find it a bit light and jammy after the Zuccardi Malbec, though . . .

Your next stop should be across the Andes mountains in Chile, for a taste of some premium, oaky Cabernets, Merlots, Carmenères and blends – and don't forget to sample Uruguay's own signature grape, Tannat, which is richer and more tannic than our featured wine. By now you should have built up an interesting picture of South America's most powerful red wines.

Hop across to North America, then, and sample some red wines from California. Up and down the West Coast, you'll find some impressive Zinfandels too. Zin has a rich fruity quality, just like Malbecs, and we bet you find a good example that's a fine match for the Argentinian wine we used as a starting point.

If you like this, it's also highly likely that you'll love many Aussie reds, especially the plummy, juicy, smooth-yet-concentrated blends of Cabernet–Shiraz, and the new blends of Grenache, Shiraz and Mourvèdre that have started popping up recently. Australian reds typically have lots of ripe fruit and good firm structure, as do South Africa's biggest wines. From the Cape, try a medium-bodied, plummy Pinotage, or good-value, inexpensive Cabernet and Cabernet blends.

New Zealand's reds are a good comparison with Malbec – the Pinot Noirs will be anyway, though do try some of the reds from warmer spots like Hawke's Bay and Waiheke Island for a few excellent, ripe Merlot–Cabernet blends and fine Syrah.

What about Europe? You can find similar ripe, intense, slightly spicy flavours, but you need to look in warmer-climate areas. In France, that means the Rhône Valley and the Deep South. Look out for Syrah-based reds with bags of blackcurrant and pepper. Of course, you must try the wines made around Cahors for a taste of Malbec, French-style!

Southern Italy is another good source of big-hearted, fruit-packed, slightly savoury reds – try wines from Sicily in particular, and especially the Syrah/Shiraz and local grape varieties being made there. Sample the southern Italian grape varieties Nero d'Avola, Primitivo and Negroamaro in particular, as they often have a similar mix of ripe, rounded fruit and spicy notes.

Look to Spain for up-and-coming regions like Campo de Borja, Toro and Jumilla making good-value, easy-drinking but ripe reds to rival Argentinian Malbec. And don't forget

Portugal – the reds now emerging from regions like Alentejo and Ribatejo have similar qualities – plenty of modern flavours, an easy-drinking, ripe, rounded fruitiness, and great value for money. Crack these wines open with lamb chops, sausage rolls, pizzas and meaty pasta sauces, cheesy vegetable bakes, even medium-spicy red meat curries.

Vintages

The whole subject of 'vintage' wine versus 'non-vintage' can sound a bit mysterious, but it needn't be. A 'vintage' wine (one with a specific year on the label) simply means it comes from just that one year. Non-vintage wines can be made with the produce of different years blended together. A non-vintage Champagne, for example, might well be made mainly from the fruit of a recent crop, but with some older wine blended in to give extra depth and richness. A vintage Champagne, however, should only be made in a very good year, from the grapes of that one single year, sold after three years' ageing. Other rules are attached to other wines – vintage port, for example, is considered the best and most complex port of all, and is made only in very good years, bottled young and needing long cellaring before it's ready. As for ordinary, inexpensive table wines, you really don't need to worry too much about which vintage you pick, or indeed whether you pick a non-vintage wine. In particular, New World wine countries and hotter spots like southern Italy or France, with their generally reliable climates, make oceans of palatable, tasty, affordable wine in almost every year. Start to buy premium wine, though, especially from a notoriously 'difficult' region like Burgundy, and it pays to look into vintages more closely, perhaps getting hold of the latest 'at a glance' pocket guide to the subject before splashing out.

The Rest of the 'New' Wine World

Apart from the 'big six' New World wine countries in the last chapters, there are other parts of the globe that deserve a mention. One of the most inspiring things about wine is the way new areas keep coming along, wowing us with their latest contributions to the wide range of styles on offer. After all, each addition to the shelves brings with it a new 'take' on the subject, either a different grape variety or a fresh stance on an old favourite.

The following countries are all playing their part in the 21st century – if you get the chance to try their wines, then jump at it. What may be a problem is finding these bottles – not many of the countries featured below have a strong presence in the UK. But the scene is constantly evolving, so keep an eye out at the wine merchants, and we'll be doing regular updates with the Wine Club, so check out the website.

Canada

'Isn't it too cold to make wine in Canada?' – the winemakers of the country's two important grape growing regions must get heartily sick of hearing this question. The answer is a resounding 'no' – not in British Columbia, anyway, where the Okanagan Valley is practically desert in parts! Here, and from Vancouver Island, expect decent, ripe Pinot Noir, Pinot Gris, Merlot and Chardonnay. Further east, in Ontario, some fine reds, Rieslings and Chardonnays are made. The most exciting Canadian wine, however, is super-sweet Icewine, made from autumnal and winter grapes which have frozen and thawed several times on the vine, creating concentrated juice for intense, luscious, zestily fresh pudding wine – delectable.

Uruguay

South America is a fascinating place for wine at the moment, with the established and critically renowned bottles of Chile, the dynamic progress of Argentina and the new kid on the block – the Tannat grape from Uruguay. Never heard of it? You soon will and once tasted, Tannat is rarely forgotten. The name of this grape almost sounds tannic, and sure enough, Tannat makes thick, beefy reds, deeply coloured and somewhat tough in character. The best examples are softer than usual, with plenty of concentrated mulberry and bramble fruit, but a more rounded, easy-to-enjoy texture. Tannat is sometimes blended with other red grapes, like Cabernet and Merlot. Also look out for Chardonnay, Sauvignon Blanc and Viognier from this country in the future.

Brazil

Brazilian wine is even rarer than Uruguay's brands at the moment. Still, a handful of companies have started exporting to our shores in recent years and we can expect more in the future. Most of the wine comes from the south of the country, where some promising reds and sparkling wines seem to be the pick of the crop. As with so many emerging wine regions, talented winemakers from around the world are flying in to grab a share of the action, and their words of wisdom are helping improve quality no end.

Mexico

If it's too cold to make wine in much of Canada, then it is too hot in most of Mexico! That said, cooler coastal areas, especially Baja California, are enjoying success now, making typically bright, fruity, clean-tasting wines from Cabernet Sauvignon, Chardonnay and other grapes. Look out for L.A. Cetto's Petite Syrah – Mexico's best-known red. The future looks promising here.

Israel

Time was when Israel only produced medium-sweet, pasteurised kosher wine, but now a new wave of modern, better-quality table wines is emerging, often from small, highly dedicated young wineries. The best regions are Galilee and Shomron. Bordeaux-style reds lead the way.

Lebanon

There's one famous, critically acclaimed winery in the Lebanon, Château Musar, which has been going for over seventy-five years. It makes a pleasing, long-lived red blend which has a leathery, spicy quality as well as ripe, rich fruit. There are several other wineries too – the best wines are from the Bekaa Valley region, where almost all the wine grapes in the Lebanon are grown and where conditions are ideal for creating premium wine. French grapes Grenache, Cinsault, Syrah and Carignan are most prolific.

America

California completely dominates the American wine industry, but it is worth saying a few words about the other wines made there. In fact, almost every American state attempts some winemaking – but only three are truly important. These are: New York State, where powerful whites and reds are made on Long Island and sparkling wines and Rieslings from the Finger Lakes area have been popular for a long time; Washington State, where vibrant, juicy, modern wines are turned out from irrigated hot, semi-desert areas – reds are best; and Oregon, perhaps the most interesting, for its complex and serious Pinot Noirs, Pinot Gris and Riesling, the best of which taste almost like top European examples from France and Germany. When Oregon's wines are good, they are very good, owing to the cool climate here, but they can suffer in some vintages.

China

China has lots of vineyards – a little-known fact, but one that will become apparent when Chinese wines start to appear more regularly here, as they certainly will do. At the moment, the vast majority of Chinese bottles are cracked open in the country itself, and you'll only spot the occasional example on the wine list in a Chinese restaurant (usually Tsingtao Chardonnay, a generously fruity white). But overseas' winemakers are showing an interest in China, and new vineyards are being developed all the time, especially in the coastal provinces of Shandong, Hebei and Tianjin. Cabernet Sauvignon, Chardonnay and Riesling are the most promising grapes.

Morocco

Not strictly speaking a 'new' wine country, as Morocco has made wine for a very long time, but exciting new bottles have started appearing in our shops for the first time. Until the middle of the last century, ripe Moroccan reds were often added to French wines to thin them out! Now that's banned of course, as production laws have been tightened up. Ironically, a new era is seeing French investment in Moroccan vineyards, and some surprisingly tasty reds and rosés just starting to appear. Expect earthy leathery spicy flavours.

India

Grapes have been grown in India for thousands of years, but they are mostly sold for eating, not for fermenting into wine. You might come across the sprightly sparkling wine Omar Khayyam or a few modern whites, reds and rosés. However, the best at the moment are from Grover Vineyards. There are signs of interest from foreign winemakers in projects based in India, so there may be more to report in the next few years.

Champagne and Sparkling Wine

If you've enjoyed a glass of fizz recently, chances are you were celebrating something. It's one of the best traditions of all – cracking open a bottle of bubbly at life's really good moments. Whether you're toasting your birthday, enjoying an anniversary, raising a glass to the bride, to exam results, or to a happy new year, somehow it's just got to be sparkling wine or Champagne to make the occasion feel really special.

And it does the trick. That's partly because of the lovely ritual of opening the bottle – untwisting the wire cage round the top, and getting a 'pop' out of the cork, then pouring the hissing fizz into the glasses. It also feels exciting to drink these wines because they are immediately refreshing, with clean, crisp flavours and those wonderful, joyous bubbles bursting on the tongue. The alcohol is delivered to your system more quickly, too, because the bubbles mean there is more surface area for the wine to be absorbed in the stomach faster. Sparkling wines are not more powerfully alcoholic than other wines, but they do take effect more suddenly!

Then there's the fact that fizz tends to cost more, and comes with fancy labels – it has a certain image, a raised kudos. There's certainly nothing like ordering a bottle of Champagne in a restaurant if you're out to impress! Friends can be sure you've spent a fortune, at any rate. And there's the point – most sparkling wine, but especially Champagne, is very expensive compared with still wine. So is it worth it, and do you have to buy pricey Champagne when there are alternatives?

You might not even know what the difference is – many people find the whole subject of fizz very confusing, and no wonder, when 'Champagne' is still incorrectly used too often as a general term. The fact is, Champagne is only Champagne when it comes from the Champagne region of north-east France. The cool climate and chalky soils here, plus the meticulous traditional method of making the sparkling wine in this region, and its strict rules and regulations mean that the best Champagnes are, indeed, utterly irresistible, with wonderful elegance, fresh, fruity flavours and a rich, yeasty-creamy note.

Method? The base wine is fermented for a second time in the bottle, and the carbon dioxide gas that results is trapped in the wine. The dead yeast from this second fermentation forms a creamy deposit which is left in the bottle for some time. Ageing the wine on its yeast sediment gives it extra richness and creaminess – a bready, yoghurty character. Eventually the sediment is removed and the bottle topped up and resealed with the wide cork and that distinctive wire cage.

But this method is not unique to Champagne – it is now used by good sparkling wine producers around the world. (It's called the 'methode traditionnelle', words to look out for on a label when choosing quality bubbly.) And the competition is hotting up. Let's be honest, most cheap 'bargain' Champagne is usually disappointing, with tart acidity and little fruity flavour. Our message is, if you want to buy really great, memorable sparkling wine, then by all means splash out on a top Champagne (either vintage or non-vintage, but older vintage Champagnes from the well-known 'houses' are generally the most delicious). Expect to pay £20 plus. At around £15 you may be lucky – the supermarket own-label Champagnes are surprisingly tasty at this price point, though don't expect great finesse. But if your budget is around a tenner, then it's better to look outside of the Champagne region for brilliant bubblies.

That means the New World wine countries, where bright, vivacious, frothy fizz can offer value for money. Try a sparkler from Australia, New Zealand or California, as we think these are the best buys. Cool-climate vineyards are the top areas for sparkling wine grapes – to get that crisp, refreshing edge, the base wine must have high acidity, and you get that from cool-climate fruit. Even England is now making some award-winning sparkling wine now, so you can see how handy a cooler climate can be for this wine style.

If you plan on spending around a fiver, then Spain's classic sparkling wine, cava, is your best bet. Cava is made in the Penedes region in the north-east, from local grape varieties, but it's made by the same, careful method as Champagne. Don't look for the complex flavours and richness of Champagne but, nonetheless, cava is surprisingly reliable, fresh and appealing. That makes it fantastic value for big parties and for ordinary, everyday drinking.

Here's how to enjoy all Champagne and sparkling wine at its best. Choose a label that says 'brut' for a dry, aperitif style; 'demi-sec' for a slightly sweeter, luscious style; or go for honeyed, grapey Asti from Italy for a sparkler to serve with sweet cakes and puddings. Chill all fizz before serving. Open slowly and carefully, keeping the bottle pointed away from anyone's face, as the cork can explode suddenly and cause a nasty eye injury. Hold the bottle firmly in one hand, while gently prising out the cork with the fingers of the other hand. Aim for a gentle 'psshht', not a huge bang – that way, you won't spill much (it helps if you hold the bottle and glass at an angle). Pour slowly down the sides of tall, narrow Champagne 'flutes', the perfect shape of glass to show off the fine streams of bubbles as they rise up through the liquid. Enjoy – life doesn't get much better than this!

Here are our experts' tips on how to get the best out of fizz . . .

JOE WADSACK

In the budget camp, go for good cava, New Zealand sparkling, or Crèmant de Limoux from southern France. The important thing is that the wine has a knife-edge bite – a shiver in the glass. I prefer pin-sharp styles to broad, rich, toasty styles. But some of the supremely good Champagnes prove you can have both. The very best vintage Champagnes may have rich toasty tones but the wine still sets every hair on my body on end (yes, every one!). This is the ultimate fizz rush, and, for me, the best sort of wine in the world . . .

SUSY ATKINS

I don't think we should be so formal about sparkling wine – there are bottles to suit every occasion, not just special ones. The Aussies drink sparkling wine as regularly as every other type of wine and I think we should do the same! Sure, a fab bottle of top Champagne will cost a fortune. These wines are often sublime, but most of us will not splash out very often. Go for a different, affordable sparkler for parties and dinners – I would pick a decent, fruity Californian or New Zealand fizz to kick-start a good dinner party, and definitely choose cheap dry cava if I'm having a big bash. Use cava as a base for sparkling cocktails when there's a crowd in – I never use Champagne then, as it is just a waste of expensive bubbles. And try matching richer, creamier sparklers with food such as light savoury canapés, fresh seafood and grilled white fish.

JEAN-MARC SAUBOUA

Hardly surprising, but I like real Champagne. This must be the most difficult drink to imitate in the world. The closest is perhaps from New Zealand. Don't forget, Champagnes and sparkling wines can age well, but then again you can enjoy them at any age! When they are young, I prefer them extra dry, but I like them even more after ten or fifteen years. I drink the older ones not too cold, when they have turned a deep gold colour, lost their aggressive sparkle, and become creamier with maturity . . . that's good Champagne, but I also love simple sparklers, and I really adore sparkling rosé that tastes fruity, easy and fresh.

Index

Acknowledgments

Amanda Ross, would like to thank: Natalie Fox, Producer for tireless checking and research; Julia Bennet and Elissa Standen for setting up the New World; Keith Heddle and Alexis Prince for making sure the Wine Club never goes dry; Simon Ross for his inspiration and support; Alastair Giles for everything; everyone at HarperCollins but especially Trevor Dolby, who maintained our sense of humour no matter what, but most of all the Wine Club members whose enthusiasm made this possible.